Historical Research

POCKET GUIDES TO
SOCIAL WORK RESEARCH METHODS

Series Editor
Tony Tripodi, DSW
Professor Emeritus, Ohio State University

Determining Sample Size
Balancing Power, Precision, and Practicality
Patrick Dattalo

Preparing Research Articles
Bruce A. Thyer

Systematic Reviews and Meta-Analysis
Julia H. Littell, Jacqueline Corcoran,
and Vijayan Pillai

Historical Research
Elizabeth Ann Danto

ELIZABETH ANN DANTO

Historical
Research

OXFORD
UNIVERSITY PRESS
2008

OXFORD
UNIVERSITY PRESS

Oxford University Press, Inc., publishes works that further
Oxford University's objective of excellence
in research, scholarship, and education.

Oxford New York
Auckland   Cape Town   Dar es Salaam   Hong Kong   Karachi
Kuala Lumpur   Madrid   Melbourne   Mexico City   Nairobi
New Delhi   Shanghai   Taipei   Toronto

With offices in
Argentina   Austria   Brazil   Chile   Czech Republic   France   Greece
Guatemala   Hungary   Italy   Japan   Poland   Portugal   Singapore
South Korea   Switzerland   Thailand   Turkey   Ukraine   Vietnam

Published by Oxford University Press, Inc.
198 Madison Avenue, New York, New York 10016
www.oup.com

Oxford is a registered trademark of Oxford University Press.

Library of Congress Cataloging-in-Publication Data
Danto, Elizabeth Ann.
Historical research / Elizabeth Ann Danto.
p. cm.—(Pocket guides to social work research methods)
Includes bibliographical references and index.
ISBN 978-0-19-533306-0
1. Sociology—Research—Methodology.
2. Sociology—History. I. Title.
HM571.D36 2008
301.072'2—dc22
2008012837

For Arthur

Acknowledgments

Last year at this time, a book on historical research methods in social work was altogether unlikely. But today, thanks to Tony Tripodi's initiative as series editor and Irwin Epstein's foresight, it is here. The enthusiasm for scholarship spread by Jacqueline B. Mondros, dean of the Hunter College School of Social Work, and by Michael Frabricant, director of the PhD program in Social Welfare, is unmistakable. So too is the support of my wonderful colleagues and students at Hunter College and the Graduate Center of the City University of New York, of Maura Roessner and Mallory Jensen at Oxford University Press, and of my husband and best friend, Paul Werner. The camaraderie and confidence of Theresa Aiello, Heide Estes, and Clark Sugg helped immeasurably, as did Amy Darden Amos's exemplary talents as a research assistant. Finally I thank my father, Arthur C. Danto, for his relentless commitment to the life of the mind.

Contents

Historical Research

Introduction

Historiography

The villagers are watching a play about the history of England. Suddenly we are in the nineteenth century. "Colonel Mayhew did not dispute the producer's right to skip two hundred years in less than fifteen minutes. But the choice of scenes baffled him. 'Why leave out the British Army? What's history without the Army, eh?' he mused. Inclining her head, Mrs. Mayhew protested after all one mustn't ask too much." On the contrary, Virginia Woolf seems to say in *Between the Acts*, we must ask and ask and ask.

We ask questions about history so that our choice of scenes is less baffling, so that we don't skip two hundred years without a reason, and so that we can know that we can never ask too much. What follows is a handbook on how to ask questions about history.

What Is Historiography in Social Work?

Some of the most exciting social work is written as history. Jane Addams's memoirs of Hull House or Abramovitz's chronicle of the lives of poor women in Colonial America give flavor to the reality of clinical and social welfare policy work. Yet the rich realities they describe are developed systematically and accord with generally accepted methodological principles. *Historiography* is the term used to describe the method of doing historical research. Purposefully collecting historical data is just one component of historiography. "When you study 'historiography,' you do not study the events of the past directly, but the changing interpretations of those events in the works of individual historians .... The method is the study of the way history has been and is written," as Furay and Salevouris (1988, p. 223) define it. In other words, historiography in social work is not history itself, but the systematic process of doing the history. The direct study of "events of the past" appeals to those with an empirical bent, but the more compelling possibility posed by the study of "changing interpretations" is that we all hold an incredible range of historical narratives that remain locked away under normal circumstances. This view of historiography allows us to expose the stories that are buried—often not consciously—within books, families, political organizations, social classes, and icons of culture. Exploring how history is written gives us access to these known and unknown areas of the world.

Historiography falls into a number of distinct areas. One field looks at how the academic discipline of history developed in different cultures and at different epochs—that is, how and why a body of historical writing was produced during a specific time concerning a specific topic. For instance, "social work historiography during the 1960s" means the methodological approaches and ideas about the history of social work that were developed during the decade of the 1960s. A second area of historiography is formed by the application of particular methods, approaches, techniques, and guidelines with which researchers collect evidence systematically in order to develop a defensible historical narrative. A third but equally adventurous historiographic focus looks at the profound debates regarding how and where social work started (in truth, its very nature), how it progressed, and where it stands today. No profession in the United States has a broader perspective on human needs than social work. Bold but also functional, social work distinctively places the pursuit of social justice on a par with the clinical treatment of individuals, pairs and families. Yet for much of the twentieth century, proponents of macro and micro approaches to practice have challenged each other's commitment to social progressivism and humanist values. Historical studies that explore this perennial debate might delve into such fascinating areas as the origin of the welfare state, the impact of slavery, the "children's rights" perspective in child welfare as compared to the "family preservation" ideology, or the fundamental nature-versus-nurture deliberations in mental health.

Historiography in social work has similarities to and differences from, for example, historiography in medieval English or quantum physics. Unlike these other areas, the social work history investigator must pursue two threads simultaneously: one that presents social work as a practice that responds to clients within the ongoing functioning of the social service agency, and another that places this practice within the larger (even global) political, linguistic, and cultural contexts of the agency's community. Like all historiography, a historical study in social work requires decisions on how best to conduct the research.

The historical imagination is vast, but an individual study is defined by the inclusion of certain methodological fundamentals: definition of a problem, testable hypothesis (or an equivalent research question), definition of the variables, gathering and analysis of historical data, and interpretation of the findings. The study must pose good scholarly questions and then attempt to respond to these questions by analyzing evidence that has been collected systematically. Reliability and validity must be factored into historical studies in social work. As in the historiography of other academic disciplines, data are collected from four types of historical evidence: primary sources (original documents, generally held by public and private archival collections), secondary sources (the work of other scholars writing about history), running records (agency reports, case notes), and recollections (autobiographies, memoirs, oral history). In addition, realia, or artifacts (including architecture, maps, objects, specimens, artwork), enhance the credibility of the historical study.

The issues of context (culture, community, origin), construction (subjectivity, narratives, migrations), contingency (time, place), and competence (individual or collective assets, resilience) have become progressively more significant over the last few decades. So too has critical thinking; among new systems of thought, postmodern and multicultural methodologies have given social workers deeper and richer insights into the lived experience of earlier generations, especially of disenfranchised and marginalized groups. "The postmodern movement has had a dramatic influence on social work," wrote Joan Laird in 1995. "It is too early to know how widespread this paradigmatic shift will be.... Nevertheless, it is forcing a re-examination of some of social work's long and dearly held assumptions." Historiography, with its far-reaching scope and methodological depth, moves this reexamination forward. As such, it is exceptionally useful for both the study and the teaching of social welfare policy, human behavior in the social environment, clinical and community practice and, of course, research.

Significance of the Method for Social Work Research

The writing of history in social welfare and social science, with its fervent hunts through slave narratives, immigrant folklore, and urban tales, promotes intriguing scholarship from child welfare to psychoanalysis. Social work scholars employ many frames of reference in order to construct this knowledge. These frames include but are not limited to ethnic background, race, class, gender, sexual orientation, ability, language usage, and religious, cultural, and political identities. The potential for knowledge construction depends very much on how we attempt to include these various frames in our research. Properly executed, a historical study can bring together a number of them and create an intersectional perspective. How do race and class intersect in a study of slave narratives, for example? Can we find intersecting points of gender and politics in a study of welfare rights organizing?

The challenge is to find genuinely meaningful approaches to the study of the past. To do this, we can look through any one of the various new frames, or lenses, and find a new context in which to understand a historical subject or event. The narrative of Jane Addams's life and work, for example, lends itself to multiple strands of inquiry: the history of

women and gender (the feminist lens and the gender lens), the construction and deconstruction of the language of charity (the postmodern
lens), the chronological history of the settlement house movement
(empirical historiography). Each one of these has far-reaching possibilities and significance for historical research and writing.

Results of historical studies are quite practical: they can form blueprints for contemporary social service programs or models for community development, or they can influence clinical approaches to work with
individuals or families. For example, universal access to health care (and
of the place of mental health services within a universal framework) is
being debated on every level of government today. Do citizens have a
social right to mental health care regardless of their ability to pay? A historical study that points to the themes in the success or failure of attempts
at universal health care in the 1960s may contain interesting implications
for addressing this public policy issue; it can also organize a number of
frames of reference, in this case social class, ability, and culture. The press
for affordability is an increasingly dominant political issue among organized providers of mental health services today. Thus it would be important to ascertain if consumers/clients as well as providers have historically
found the universal health care experience adequate, effective, and equi-
table. In this way, a historically based analysis has potential for application to program planning.

Finally, historical studies often provide new evaluative strategies from
the standpoint of an agency's shifting concerns for service and its political responses over the decades. As such, historiographic scholarship can
have a sizeable role in understanding the social work profession from a
number of ideological and economic dimensions. Exploring why, for
example, American physicians of the 1960s apparently chose *not* to sub-
scribe to universal health care like their European contemporaries should
shed light on the development of, and obstacles to, the delivery of social
services today.

This book is written first and foremost for the community of doctoral candidates in social work. I anticipate, however, that a broad range
of scholars in the social and behavioral sciences will find it useful. In
particular, social work and social science educators for whom no book on

historiography has been written will now have access to a text on historical research methods from which they can draw lecture notes, guidelines
for historical studies, and a lively pedagogy. The author of such a study
needs to explain technical concepts and their significance, but also be
excited by the idea that writing history is an interpretive exercise.
Academics in social work find historical research both challenging and
rewarding because it purposely raises the context and cultural developments out of which a client base emerges. Furthermore, it does so in a
way that increases the respect given social workers, whose profession is
often associated with seemingly intransigent human problems, client
transience, and caution bred of institutionalized racism, sexism, and
other paradigms of stigma.

Historical research in social work has a distinctive chronicle itself. At
least since the 1950s, history has found a curious niche in the social work
canon, based largely on its concern for the past within a present-centered
profession. The interdisciplinary Social Welfare History Group, a joint
endeavor of professional historians and social workers, fluctuated in
tandem with the American political economy (Fisher, 1999). Yet the social
services are, and have always been, sites in which the social workers'
uniquely empowering skill set, ethical standards and collaborative strategies have been profoundly influential at the federal, state and local levels.
Robert Barker's *Milestones in the Development of Social Work and Social
Welfare* (1998) provides the profession with a good perspective on its history. Robert Fisher's 1999 study of the place of historical research in social
work explores the incidence, persistence, and marginalization of historical research in social work by examining one indicator, social work dis-
sertations. Despite the dominance of other methods, historical research
has a solid tradition as a legitimate method for doctoral research in social
work. Nevertheless, "the current state of historical research seems terribly
myopic," Fisher and Dybicz write (1999, p. 105), "especially given developments in other social science disciplines and challenges to contemporary social work research." Fortunately, this is an eminently correctable
situation.

Today the standard rhetoric—building on client strengths, creating
community, educating for empowerment—assumes new complexities.

Attempts to resolve the perennial power differential between social worker and client, oppressor and oppressed, or teacher and student are often obscured by social, cultural, and linguistic gaps. From the very beginning of a historical research project, excitement over a past event and its present consequences should influence the researcher's thinking about the costs and benefits of deep research into long-gone lives and ways of life. The need to embrace the variety of history—to learn and to teach how each group has negotiated power—is writ large.

In Sum

Historical writing can be deceptively simple, beginning with a single document or a journal, but it is never a straightforward string of facts. It is very different from quantitative analysis or natural science writing. The researcher must patiently filter documents through an understanding of the original authors, where they come from, and how their stories changed over time. For this reason, this book includes a database of archival resources and guidelines for research in archives, as well as special protocols for American Indian archives. On one hand, a great deal of attention is paid to details, since physical elements of the documents (such as penmanship or paper quality) as well as language usage can reflect social class, environment, education, and socioeconomic status. On the other hand, one must never lose sight of the document's overarching narrative, in which the details are situated. Regardless of their artistic or monetary value, documents always offer fascinating, if unintended, historical correlates. Also, since so much of history is held in nontraditional forms, guidelines for conducting culturally sensitive oral history interviews are included in this book.

Within the following chapters you will find mentioned a number of important works on social work and social welfare history, to which Roy Lubove's *The Professional Altruist: The Emergence of Social Work as a Career, 1880–1930* and *The Struggle for Social Security, 1900–1935* can be added. James Leiby's vintage attempt at a major synthesis, *A History of Social Welfare and Social Work in the United States*, and Leslie Leighninger's

Social Work: Search for Identity also provide excellent reference material. What you will not find here, however, is a comprehensive review of the literature on the history of social work and social welfare, nor that history itself. Start writing, please.

At the beginning of her nuanced memoir, the Cairo physician Nawal El Saadawi protests: "When I sit down to write, it is the small household tasks, the sound of the doorbell or the telephone, which torture me." The ironic correlation here is that the "torture" lies not in this personal detail but in the overall political environment; it is an audible symbol of an intellectual's 1981 imprisonment for "attack[ing] the ruling system," the violent repression and social disintegration perpetrated in Egypt under Anwar Sadat. This kind of anecdote is relevant to social work history because, like the profession itself, our multidimensional focus on human diversity is one of our greatest strengths. Social work is a proving ground for a global multicultural society, a democratic profession set up just over one hundred years ago to expand the reach of government toward citizens failed by other institutions. Few American professions have a more dramatic story.

1

Historiographic Approaches

"Could it be that in history, as in all areas of human knowledge, we are finally ready to concede that there is no single history, no total system, that will encompass and explain all we want to know?" asks Nicole Eustace (2003, p. 77). While historians constantly disagree over why events come about and how to study them, a series of informed approaches, or new lenses, have emerged since the mid-1960s to describe methods of investigating how history happens. Each methodological approach has a set of distinguishing features, but all attempt to reexamine new and old sources in light of a particular contemporary objective—that of bringing to light the everyday lives of ordinary people. Researchers, scholars, and interpreters of history select an approach that best suits their political ideology, and then explore cultural relationships and place the past within the world of humanistic studies. The approaches described in this chapter are empirical (descriptive), social, cultural, feminist, postmodern, postcolonial, and selected subsets of each. They do overlap, and the researcher's choice should be driven by an imperative to employ the most exciting images, the most evocative narratives, and—inevitably—the approaches that are the most personally relevant.

Empirical or descriptive historiography assures us that recorded facts are paramount and that readers and academic consumers share their concern about accuracy. *Social* historiography too is empirical in nature; its well-disciplined focus stays on social categories and the behavioral tendencies of groups (but not individuals). In contrast, *cultural* historiography urges us to curtail our fixation on facts as objective reality and to begin serious discussions about the influence of social constructions, including the overriding role of culture, on historical events as subjective experience. The *feminist* approach holds that in order to counteract masculinist ascendance in history, historiography should systematically ask how women experienced, developed, or recorded events—or not. In *postmodern* historiography, traditional textual research methods are subjected to intense intellectual scrutiny in an attempt to uncover more nuanced explanations of power relations and the multiplicity of social and political behaviors. The *postcolonial* approach has yet a different view: it provides us with a logic with which to abate the dominance of traditionally oppressive racial and economic governments over history. *Marxist* historiography stands in stark contrast to the linearity of empirical work, and *quantitative* historiography can either stand alone or be integrated into any number of other approaches. Of course, internal reliability and external validity are vital to any study, regardless of the chosen historiographic approach.

Empirical Historiography

Empirical historiography is based on the "descriptive history" model proposed by G. R. Elton (1965), who argues that the "historical method is no more than a recognized and tested way of extracting from what the past has left the true facts and events of that past." Elton was opposed to analysis and contextual explanation, and he was aligned with the positivist tradition of research. Positivists generally assume that reality is an objective "given" that can be described with scientific precision by independent measures, instruments, and observers (researchers), all of which are value-free. Descriptive history makes use of interesting forms of quantitative research, including formal statistical and mathematical methods, to produce warrantable knowledge and, in contrast to contemporary interpretive approaches to data collection, tends to be viewed as valuable but too deterministic. At their best, descriptive historical narratives are full of lively details and vivid scenery, and should help the reader picture the original situation in which an event took place.

Then again, many people take part in the creation of an event, and the representation of "facts" is far from free of value judgments. For example, even a purely descriptive history of a particular book's progress from manuscript to distribution of the printed book demands an account of the many aesthetic and economic decisions made along the way. A good study should convey the idea of this flow. There are legendary writers, illustrators, and type designers, trade and noncommercial paper makers, binders and printers, and a publishing house whose staff can add to (or thwart) the writer's intentions. Postproduction, wholesale and retail booksellers, librarians, and book purchasers or library readers all have their say in the book's distribution. All of these individuals and groups ultimately influence the path of the physical book, and each one should be set apart in a descriptive history of the route.

Descriptive history is, then, the close physical description of events. How was the event assembled day to day, even hour to hour? What sorts of documents were used to describe it and who wrote them? Was the event illustrated in pictures, and of what kind? Where are the illustrations maintained and how? Who remembers the event, and under what circumstances? In order to give us a complete objective description of a person or event's physical appearance accurately and economically, the author of a descriptive history must use scientific precision, be determined to get all the details right, and quote all sources scrupulously. These displays of exact scholarship often contrast and compare documents along a timeline, enabling us to distinguish one specific event from another and to identify significant variations within a single event. Good descriptive histories are therefore indispensable to social workers, whatever their fields of interest and whatever the time period their studies cover. Since traditional descriptive histories do not exist for all fields and for all periods, especially histories of disenfranchised groups and controversial events, social workers should make a particular effort to recapture previously ignored data.

EXAMPLE: In *Empiricism and History*, Stephen Davies explains what historians mean by empiricism, examines the origins, growth, and persistence of empirical methods, and shows how students can apply these methods to their own work. Clarke A. Chambers and Peter Romanovsky's still-classic *Social Service Organizations* (1978) provides a concise narrative on the history and activities of nearly two hundred "national and local voluntary social service agencies that have been part of American social work," drawing on data from archives, annual reports, and other sources.

Microhistory, the study of the past on a very small scale, emerged in the 1960s as an interesting new technique of empirical historiography with cultural overtones. In contrast to the "grand narratives"—the "enormously influential encyclopedic works," as Magnússon (2006, p. 907) writes—"the ideology of the 'singularization of history' is grounded in the fact that it is impossible to know more than a tiny fragment of the story, that the sources preserve only a minute selection of the moments, and that if the compass is increased our possibilities of attaining an understanding of what has happened decrease still further." This ideology suggests that the experience of many can be captured in the case of one. Placing a historical moment under a microscope, as it were, offers the kind of intimate examination of human connections rarely found in broad cultural histories. Most types of microhistories are case studies of particular small towns or villages, or single clinics or agencies, and are based on the idea that major events are rooted in individual actions within organizations or communities. Some are studies of an individual deemed to be of minor importance until now, and most share an empirical reliability traditionally associated with the fields of anthropology and sociology. Consequently, microhistory studies have much larger ramifications (in contrast to local history, written solely for its inherent interest to the local community) and have influenced researchers who believe in generalizing historical trends from case studies.

EXAMPLE: When Michael Lorenzini, a curator at the Municipal Archives of the City of New York, decided to examine a certain collection of images, he realized that all twenty thousand images, on glass negatives and prints, had been created by a single unknown person. An employee of the city's Department of Bridges from 1903 to 1934 had recorded in forceful photographs the city's infrastructure as it grew: subway tunnels, ferries, trolley lines, the Manhattan and Queensboro bridges, the Municipal Building. The employee's name was Eugene de Salignac, who was virtually unknown until Lorenzini researched his work and wrote it up as a microhistory. From *New York Rises*, we can generalize about urban development, social policy reflecting the employment and displacement of New York's immigrants, and the challenges inherent in reconciling the exploitation and grand visions inherent in American modernism.

Social History

As a defined method, social historiography has given us many of the analytical tools we use for doing systematic research. These tools (gauging the reliability and validity of evidence, clear definition of a historical problem, a theoretical framework or hypothesis, questions about social roles and functions) also provide a framework with which we can appraise the value of historical research. As a result, writers of social history are often involved in exhaustive research efforts and find themselves doing a kind of detective work, tracking down enough original documents, objects, and records (such as census tracts, court records, and newspaper indexes) to describe what few people, if any, have thought worthy of historical attention before. The historical event is the nucleus of the study, one where the individual's social status is determined by a group situation and placed within the machinery of a social category. The fact that historical events may be presented as closed and polished does not make social history any less valuable—it has given us labor history, with its focus on the experiences of workers, women, and racial minorities; urban history; and other histories of African Americans, the family, children, medicine, social classes, and more.

Social histories cull their narratives from large amounts of systematic historical evidence to track how social norms, behaviors, and social trends developed. Elements from the politics and economics of a society are synthesized so that individual experience may be placed within a broad purview. Do people follow or create social rules? Does status derive from power, or does conventional power assign status? These sorts of questions are tremendously helpful to social workers who are confronted every day by so-called deviant behavior and who have to try to locate that behavior within the individual, the individual's social groups, or more likely a combination of the two.

EXAMPLE: *The Social History of Social Work: The Issue of the "Problem Family," 1940–70*, by John Welshman, looks at evolving attitudes toward the "problem family" of the 1950s as a means of exploring the history of British social work between 1940 and 1970 through the eyes of four different interest groups (the Eugenics Society, the Pacifist Service Units, the Medical Officers of Health, and a broad coalition of academics and practitioners in professional social work). Welshman concludes that tracing the idea of the "problem family" reveals how social work professionals diverged from, but maintained close links with, other professional groups.

Cultural History

For many people writing history today, the historiographic approach the writer takes to the evidence is more meaningful than the individual historical facts, so that the facts become useful in the process of assembling a historical narrative. Cultural historiography as a method is concerned with the whole study of a historical event: its descriptive history, of course, but also the influence of the multi-layered cultural systems in which the event occurred. So, for example, the equipment of the cultural historian focusing on social work includes both a profound knowledge of the event being described (and of its era) and the ordinary people who participated in it, and an equally profound knowledge of social work theory and agency practices of that era.

The cultural historian Carl Schorske's new book *Thinking with History—Explorations in the Passage to Modernism* mixes an empiricist's precision with cultural interpretations. Schorske is fascinated by the manner in which ideas about history reflects the times and attitudes of those who lived that history. Setting out to locate ways of 19th-century thinking that led to 20th-century modernism, Schorske attempts to look at group behavior (as a social historian would) while also drawing on the experience of individuals. As practiced by Schorske and others, the cultural model of historiography explores broader cultural forces, such as the media or gender patterns, while also trying to shed new light on individual experience. It attempts to trace the relationship between an event as portrayed in a descriptive history and that event as conceived by those who experienced it. This relationship is often difficult to decipher; informants make occasional mistakes, and record keepers may have any number of biases.

Cultural history today explores popular ceremonies, local traditions, distinctive ways of living, indigenous interpretations of historical experience, and the written and oral descriptions of knowledge, customs, and arts. Music, dance, sports, television, fads and fashion, education, technology, and architecture are some of the domains of the cultural historian. So too are major events that somehow transform the culture. For instance, in 1954 Senator Joseph McCarthy began televised hearings into alleged Communists in the U.S. Army; in 1955, the American Federation of Labor and the Congress of Industrial Organizations merged, making the new AFL-CIO an organization with 15 million members; and in the same year Dr. Jonas Salk developed a vaccine for polio. Social categories that were once considered too small, too obscure, or statistically not significant are now brought into the history writer's scope; in fact, the subsidiary quality of that category is now viewed as marginalization, itself a reflection of the dominant cultural paradigm. For example, are women artists a small category? Reading most art history books, one would think so. Or are women artists an underrepresented social category because they fall outside of the masculinist norm? This is where cultural history tries to develop an alternative—and frequently more accurate—reading of historical evidence.

In newer types of cultural historiography—feminist, postcolonial, and textual, all interrelated but distinct—underlying each lens through which the past is viewed is the basic assumption that every person is embedded in a matrix formed by multiple categories of identity and power, including but not limited to race, class, and gender. No two people are ever identical, nor are their positions within this matrix; yet the history of each one expands our understanding of the matrix. Each approach carries equal weight in our understanding of people and events, though different ideological lenses appeal to different history writers depending on their own view of—and situation within—the matrix. History writing should further our understanding of the social, cultural, and political transformations that have shaped the world as we know it and, as a consequence, ourselves as individuals. If we believe that the past is a record of the multiple dimension of human experience, then researching history can add depth to our efforts to address contemporary social problems.

Feminist, Gender-Based, and Queer Historiography

"For centuries history was written in an authoritative, detached voice, communicating an illusion of logical progression, objectivity, completeness," writes the American historian Nina Rattner Gelbart (1998, p. 9). "It claimed to have discovered 'how things really were,' to be scientific and factual, and to present a linear, seamless tale. Recently such empiricist presumptions of certainty have been attacked; recovery of the past once and for all, the 'whole story,' now seems a naive and strange conceit." Indeed, today many social work researchers have reservations about the hegemonic historical narrative. The dominant social groups that hold sway over current systems of expression (the news media, for example) may appear to speak for the disenfranchised or groups of "others." In so doing, these groups (women, people of color, immigrants, etc.) are often constructed as marginal to the mainstream "center" of society. Conventional social histories have all too often discounted the views and experiences of "others," almost as if they neither existed nor affected the course of historical events. As a result, broad new categories of history writing have emerged to challenge and counteract this marginalization.

Mimi Abramovitz (1996) energetically questioned the assumption of gender neutrality in social welfare history and wrote the "long untold story of the relationship between women and the welfare state." Similarly, public historians expand on the methods of academic history by emphasizing nontraditional evidence (oral histories, photographs, films, multimedia, performance, and experimental narratives): a history of slavery drawn from slave narratives sounds very different from the same history written by plantation owners.

Feminist historiography is a specific and valid focus that consciously attributes meaning and value to the lives of women in historical narratives. Looking at events through a feminist lens leads us to question the assumptions underlying accepted historical traditions and to challenge time-honored scholarship. Documentary reconstruction is often necessary in order to make women visible as active and influential agents within narratives that have been written, consciously or not, about the male experience from the male perspective. In traditional history, women remained in their conventionally assigned gender roles and were rarely included in narratives on society such as foreign and domestic policy, industrial growth, or politics. Fortunately, much of this changed in the mid-1970s with Joan Kelly-Godal's watershed essay "The Social Relation of the Sexes: Methodological Implications of Women's History." She suggested that by looking at social change in relation to women's liberation or repression, one could "restore women to history"—that is, question socially accepted (masculinist) ideas about history and reveal previously hidden, subjugated, or marginalized knowledge. For this reason, it is important for researchers concentrating on social work (after all, about 70% of social workers are women) to reexamine historical narratives, concepts, and chronologies in order to grapple with the masculinist historical canon.

In what is now a classic of feminist history, *Regulating the Lives of Women: Social Welfare Policy from Colonial Times to the Present*, Mimi Abramovitz (1996) provides a critical historical analysis of U.S. social welfare policy and argues that the "feminization of poverty" is not a recent development but dates back to colonial times, and that rules and regulations of key social welfare programs (Social Security, AFDC, and unemployment insurance) have always been ideologically based, related to the assignment of homemaking and child care responsibilities to women.

In the mid-1990s, some writers declared feminist history outdated, and decided to direct their analyses toward a more inclusive concept of gender. Joan Wallach Scott, for example, promoted a new view that gender, rather than women, is more practical because it pertains to all human relationships and social structures. For Scott, predefined categories of race, sex, social class, or ethnicity limit our ability to historicize human experience. Her 1991 "project of making experience visible" attempts to counter "the workings of the ideological system itself [and] its categories of representation (homosexual/heterosexual, man/woman, black/white) as fixed immutable identities." Gender is conceptualized as a historically specific social construction of attributes categorized by sex, and relates as much to gender identity in men as in women. Attributes are moral, physical, behavioral, and psychological. *Gender historiography* explores the history of relations between individuals, groups, and institutions in addition to the experience and expectations of being identified as a man or as a woman.

In *Sexing the Body: Gender Politics and the Construction of Sexuality*, Anne Fausto-Sterling (2000) traces how cultural biases underlie current scientific thought on gender. She critiques the science itself, exposing historical inconsistencies in the literature, the rhetoric, and even the theoretical structures that support new research. "One of the major claims I make in this book," she explains, "is that labeling someone a man or a woman is a social decision. We may use scientific knowledge to help us make the decision, but only our beliefs about gender—not science—can define our sex. Furthermore, our beliefs about gender affect what kinds of knowledge scientists produce about sex in the first place."

As we have seen, authors of historical studies are as much a part of the stories told as the 'others' they describe. Among the newer ways of understanding what history is and how it can be written, *queer historiography* suggests that the traditional linear narrative forms of historical writing mask gender complexity and social contradictions. For this reason, representations of queer historical subjects are found in recent texts produced by lesbians and gay men of color, and they often interweave nonlinear narratives such as "autobiography, poetry, documentary material, feminist theory," (Brayman, 1997, p. 98). Queer historiography emerges from within these narratives of daily life precisely because traditional history writers have supported the heteronormative hegemony. For example, heteronormative histories of the McCarthy era fail to tell us, as D'Emilio does in his analysis of the homophile movement in the United States from 1940 to 1970, that more people lost their jobs for being allegedly homosexual than for being Communist. The process of recognizing a new historical identity involves a new approach to historiography and a clear political position on homosexuality. Likewise, this process demands that we create an original body of knowledge to convey information on the lives of those omitted or overlooked in accounts of the past, to an audience who will eventually act on it.

EXAMPLE: In the introduction to *Gay New York: Gender, Urban Culture, and the Making of the Gay Male World*, George Chauncey writes: "The gay world that flourished before World War II has been almost entirely forgotten in popular memory and overlooked by professional historians; it is not supposed to have existed" (1994, p. 22). Chauncey's use of queer historiography is twofold. He applies the empirical framework of social history to a marginalized group and carefully structures his history of how a well-defined queer population, homosexual men, lived out their lives in a single location and within a specific chronological period. Also, his work doesn't actually accuse other historians of exclusion, but the implication is clear: at this point, people who do cultural history about marginalized populations are also writing about the "normal" world in that the latter creates boundaries between itself and the stigmatized "other."

Postmodern Historiography, Public History, and Postcolonialism

In the last thirty years or so, postmodernism has had a powerful effect on the writing of history. It is difficult to reduce postmodernism to one key conceptual frame other than the postmodern position that there is no absolute or true way of representing history. Sometimes called *textual history* or *textual criticism,* the main method of postmodern history is deconstruction. Initially applied as a method of literary criticism but soon expanded to other fields, deconstruction was developed by the French philosopher Jacques Derrida. The purpose, at least with regard to historical texts, is to uncover the impact of subtle rhetorical and cultural devices that history writers employ, if unconsciously. Deconstructionists consider that a given work has multiple conflicting interpretations, and suggest that the true meaning of the work is not necessarily the meaning that the author intended. Derrida's *De la grammatologie* articulated deconstructive strategies, and since then postmodernists have expanded their perspective on human identity as fluid, mutable, and deeply connected to culture.

The French writer Michel Foucault in particular questioned the construction of social categories, finding them narrow and merely duplicative of hegemonic language and assumptions. Foucault made us aware of the social uses of power to construct dominant and subjugated categories, and that the purported "fringes" of society are so placed merely to preserve the privileged normative center. The postmodern historical criticism of Foucault and Jonathan Goldberg stands in stark contrast to modernism, the era that lasted from roughly the beginning of the twentieth century until the 1960s.

Modernism is characterized by its rejection of 19th-century positivist scholarship and by its opposition to conventional morality, taste, traditions, and economic values. At the same time, the modernist paradigm claims that social progress is inevitable and implies that, with progress, so is cultural homogeneity. This is precisely the kind of contention that slights the reality of oppression faced by nonwhites, women, poor people and other disenfranchised groups—in other words, the social work client base. "It is all too clear that what has happened is one thing, and what has been described by writers of history as having happened is quite another thing," says John Hope Franklin (1989, p. 42) in his essays on race and history. "The changes that have occurred in the writing of the history of the Negro," Franklin continues, "are as significant and in some ways, even more dramatic than the very events themselves that the writers have sought to describe." How does the client define history, community, law, and social imperative? And which definition of government or welfare, social or economic, do social workers listen to (Parton, 1994)?

Postmodernism extends these oppositions, positing a stance on human behavior that is deliberately noncategorical. Michel Foucault, for example, repudiated assumptions about individual progress and epigenetic stages of "normal" development. Instead, he asks us to examine (not to define) who we are in relation to "others," to power and authority. Although postmodernism in social work began with the admirable goal of curbing, or at least modifying, the imposition of specific cultural values, it rarely met with academic favor.

EXAMPLE: Foucault's hugely influential book *The Birth of the Clinic: An Archaeology of Medical Perception* was published in 1963 in France and translated into English in 1973. Foucault traced the historical development of the *clinique* (translated as "clinic," but here largely referring to a teaching hospital) as an institution, and by extension the medical profession. Specifically, he developed the multifaceted concept of the medical *regard* (gaze) to explore the cultural construction of dehumanization by which medical professionals separate the patient's body from the person. In another interesting example, this one specific to the social work profession, Leslie Margolin (1997) draws on a detailed examination of social work texts, primarily case histories, to argue that social work disguises its own assumptions and claims to power as a way of further legitimizing its actions.

One of the many interesting methodological venues to emerge from the postmodern movement is *narratology*. Narratology appeals to a growing constituency of oral historians for whom an individual's story at once contains deeply held cultural codes and also structures our perception of both cultural artifacts and the larger world. It asks us to explore how we sequence time and space within a narrative, for example, or even how we construct meaning in general (Harman, 2007). Given the widespread significance of narrative media today (television, film, fiction), narratology also helps us analyze the history of popular culture, and how popular culture's own historiography itself changed over time.

Of all the historiographic lenses available to social workers today, postcolonialism is particularly relevant because it grapples with the origin and ongoing oppressive effects of Eurocentrism and Americentrism as well as the legacy of colonial rule. In contrast to the nationalist perspective (perhaps unspoken or even unconscious), postcolonial writing of history vividly demonstrates the impact of dominant worldviews in the construction of social science knowledge. This legacy, combined with a bias toward market-oriented socioeconomic policies, notes the social worker Margot Breton (2002), has resulted in persistent racism in Canada and the United States. Similarly, Carlton-LaNey and Burwell (1996, p. 6) state rightly that "if social work professes to embrace diversity and an understanding of difference, it must strengthen and expand its knowledge of African American social welfare history."

If recorded history is actually the history of the elite strata of society (those who have the political power to write the history books), then the non-elite are excluded. The question is not whether such one-sidedness is unjust—history is crammed with book after book written from the perspective of privilege—but to what extent social workers can stay attuned to the disparity. Western-trained historians of the non-West have themselves at times felt oppressed by the canon of academic discourse. "The challenge of postcolonial historiography," says Tavakoli-Targhi in his effort to rebuild the history of Iran, "is to re-historicize the processes that have been concealed and ossified by the Eurocentric accounts of modernity" (2001, p. 33). Postcolonial historiography also draws attention to the personal experience of colonization, at times that of the colonized individual who acquires an identity (as insider or outsider) by confronting the institutions of those who have done the colonizing, and their larger history as well.

The method is particularly relevant given today's globalization because it takes into account how wars, for example, are rooted in long-standing power relations of imperialism and colonial advancement. Dominant, wealthy countries can take a position of "bringing civilization" to the unruly, and use state-sponsored violent practices (e.g., war) to overtake allegedly failing nations. "The United States is committed to the advance of freedom and democracy. And we have a historic objective in view," said President George W. Bush during the G8 summit of 2007. "America pursues our freedom agenda in many ways—some vocal and visible, others quiet and hidden from view." Such hegemonic rhetoric allows an American president to imagine himself as a civilizing bulwark against the violent forces of unruly and terrorist rogue states, and in a sense to accept global war and racial violence as a historical inevitability of globalization. Do earlier representations of war contribute to this construction of war as a normal function of society?

EXAMPLE: *L'Oedipe Africain* is a major text from the early years of postcolonialism and transcultural psychiatry. Psychologist Marie-Cécile Ortigues and her philosopher husband, Edmond Ortigues, produced this study after four years of clinical work (1962 to 1966) that transformed a classical asylum in Dakar, Senegal, into an open-door, culturally sensitive therapeutic center. Alice Bullard (2005) has recently reanalyzed the text to probe the controversial areas of transference in situations of racial and cultural difference, theories of the cultural *and* universal dimensions of the psyche, and the enormous assumptions we make about history, tradition, and modernity.

Even today, most historical records flow in one functional direction, from the governing establishment "down" toward the consumer. That prevents people with alternative views from disturbing the status quo. *Public history* moves in exactly the opposite direction. Constructed specifically by the voices of those who are absent from the traditional history books, it documents the human experience of social and cultural life in neighborhoods, communities, social service agencies, architectural and housing projects to name a few sites of inquiry. Sometimes called the "history of the inarticulate" (or the "new social history"), public history looks at how people encountered immigration, economic development, industrialization, crime and policing, music and entertainment, race and ethnicity, and religion in rural and urban cultures. This fairly new academic discipline—public history combines ethnography and other techniques from anthropology with oral history—seeks to produce new knowledge and widely accepted alternative official (and with any luck, more egalitarian) narratives so that we can move away from our reliance on secondary sources and on written documents deposited in archives.

Marxist Historiography

Unlike postmodernists, who question categorization of any kind, Marxist historians assert that social categories have experiential meaning in relation to each other, and also that analysis drawn from one period can be applied to others. At times called historical materialist historiography, this analytic framework is predicated on the work of Karl Marx and his theory that social class and economic imperatives determine historical outcomes. Marxist historiography takes a broad, macro view of a society, where individual units or components (families, institutions) are historical instances that reproduce the social whole. Another term used to describe this view of the nature of history as determined is *dialectical*: the subjective experience of a historical event (perceptions, arguments, and language) cannot be understood without giving equal weight to the objective (separate, distant, environmental) factors involved in creating historical outcomes. Gregor McLennan (1986, p. 94) defines what he considers to be the best in Marxist historiography: a combination of "recognition of real complexity," "commitment to the necessity of theory," and "adherence to some basic Marxist concepts."

Marxist historiography has enriched the written history of poor people and working classes, oppressed and marginalized groups and nations, and public history. The same methodology—plumbing the written and oral narratives of disenfranchised groups and assembling their history in line with dialectical principles—aims to bring forward the subjective perceptions, experiences, and interpretations of social groups that have been oppressed by mainstream history, whether by omission or by commission. For labor scholars, these analyses offer practical blueprints for energizing the U.S. labor movement by focusing attention on leadership, elitism, and social classes. Most history writers use social group categories as devices for organizing their understanding of the past, with a view to placing individual experience within the group; for Marxists, attempts at individualizing create a distraction from the overall economic pattern and "blame the victim" for a personal experience that results from large-scale economic forces, not individual deficit.

EXAMPLE: Written from the viewpoint of political economy, *From Charity to Enterprise: The Development of American Social Work in a Market Economy*, by Stanley Wenocur and Michael Reisch (2002), explores the development and professionalization of social work within this political and economic framework. This model allows the authors to examine how various subgroups within social work lost or gained control of the professional enterprise at various historical points.

Quantitative Historiography

Though the approach is not yet widespread, there is a small community of quantitative historians within academic social work. To date most historical writing and data collection has been qualitative, though on occasion our studies may be interspersed with some illustrative statistics. But with the quantitative approach, the numbers and calculations, the statistical and computer tools, become the actual springboard for depicting an event or a series or cluster of events. While all our studies investigate data and organize it with data capture instruments, quantitative historians build their studies with (usually large) databases from the outset. Even initially nonquantitative information can be quantified and then subjected to a statistical analysis as though it were a standard data set. Economic and demographic data are available in print and online in abundance. For example, major economic data sets have been collected by governments since the 1920s. Computerized census data, voting patterns, economic indicators, public opinion distribution, and home ownership all can be tracked, reorganized, and evaluated in light of a study's hypothesis. Census and other data sets can provide accurate reflections of population movements; demographics; population growth rates; rates of birth,

Household Workers Training Project, May 20, 1940, San Jose, CA. Records of
the Work Projects Administration, 1922–1944, RG 69, ARC ID 296101, U.S.
National Archives & Records Administration, Pacific Region.

death, marriage, and disease; occupational and educational distributions;
and migrations and population changes. One of the largest repositories is
the Interuniversity Consortium for Political and Social Research (ICPSR)
at the University of Michigan, which provides access to an extensive collection of downloadable political and social data for the United States
and the world.

EXAMPLE: In *Pattern and Repertoire in History* (2002), Bertrand
Roehner and Tony Syme used scientific methodology to decipher a kind
of "genetic code" of history. To illustrate how a complex and large-scale
historical event such as the French Revolution can be broken down into
clusters of occurrences that serve as building blocks for global events,
they used myriad forms of numerical evidence: a bifurcation diagram for
the Estates-General of 1789 (p. 108), historical analogies used by the U.S.
Army to develop strategies for the Vietnam war in 1965 (p. 29), and

percentages of books related to religion as compared to medical books between 1700 and 1900 (p. 91) are just a few of their tables, charts, and diagrams that quantify the components of a major historical event.

Closely related to quantitative historiography, *historiometry* is another quantitative method of analyzing statistics and measuring retrospective data. Here though, the data come from psychometric assessment of famous people, usually deceased; unlike psychobiography and psycho-history (the psychodynamics of a famous person's development), histori-ometry looks at the development of creativity, genius, and talent at the social level in populations at large. The results of both quantitative historiography and historiometry have been questioned because their near total reliance on statistics can read as poor reliability and validity.

EXAMPLE: In 2006, Dean K. Simonton set out to show that individual differences in intelligence are consistently associated with leader per-formance, including those of presidents of the United States. Given this empirical significance, he estimates IQ scores for all 42 chief executives, from George Washington to George W. Bush. The scores were obtained by applying missing-values estimation methods (expectation maximization) to published assessments of three characteristics: IQ, intellectual bril-liance, and openness to experience. The resulting scores were shown to correlate with evaluations of presidential leadership performance. The article concludes with a discussion of the implications for George W. Bush and his presidency.

2

Overall Design and Method

Historical research imparts a telescopic view of significant events within the social work profession and also a way of relating se events to their broader social context. Having selected one or more historiographic approaches with which to frame the study, the researcher also chooses among a vast array of questions to answer about a historical development in, for example, child welfare services, public education, the rise of technology and the benefits and challenges it brings, the development of practice methods, family life, sexual politics and working conditions, pioneering theoreticians in the field, government statistics, or geographical demographics and how they affect income distribution.

Logically enough, researchers need to articulate the reasons they are pursuing a study, not only for themselves but also for the communities of scholars and beyond. The *purpose* of a historical study in social work is generally twofold: (1) to provide a descriptive, longitudinal overview of specific social problems, programs, or policies within predetermined dates, and (2) to trace major ideological themes in the history of social work and its multiple ancillary fields—economics, psychoanalysis, ethnography, sociology, political science, and more—and to develop implications for practice by comparing how their different cultural and sociopolitical contexts change over time. The *rationale* for the study is to correct for gaps or misinterpretations in the published literature on this broad range of historical issues. It points to the historical (and current) impact of this gap on the administration and delivery of social services and on the education of contemporary social workers.

The Purpose of a Study

Modern writers of social work history aim to reconstruct a record of human activities within a specified time period and to achieve a deeper understanding of these activities, generally by situating them within a broad social and political context. Simply stated, the purpose of a historical study is to acquire enough evidence to support the researcher's interpretation of one or more events. It may, for example, focus on gaining insight into one aspect of the development and history of one organization, such as the specific historical factors that led to the creation of the Walter Reed Army Medical Center or the Freedman's Bureau. But on a wider scale, we may be misled into thinking that the purpose of a historical study is obvious since the content of history is stored in narratives about people and events. In fact, the record does not speak for itself—it only speaks for those who have spoken. For that reason, a study's purpose may be to recapture the voices of those who stories, problems, or situations are not so easy to check. To explore the social and ethnic upheavals of a particular era, for example, it is interesting to investigate the relationship between these historical disruptions and the development, provision, and consumption of social work services. In an era in which the term "ethnic diversity" has become commonplace, skills such as cultural competence have become familiar, if not trite. But does this sufficiently deepen our understanding of, for example, the impact of postcolonial oppression on ethnic groups? One purpose of historical studies, says Gary Cohen (1984, p. 1040), is precisely to "advance our understanding of the group psychological dimensions of ethnicity." Cohen calls intensive historical studies "indispensable" because they can systematically analyze how ethnic groups have developed, sustained, or transformed their distinctive identities in relation to their social economic and political experience. For social workers interested in clinical work with immigrant families, for example, it would be vital to understand the historical evolution of that family's group ethnic identity.

EXAMPLE: Jane Addams's clear-eyed, unsentimental memoir of twenty years as leader of Hull House, the pioneering settlement house in Chicago, has a purpose larger than a witness's report. It is an ideological record of keeping a social work project true to its mission. "Because Settlements have multiplied so easily in the Unites States," she wrote (1910, p. 2), "I hoped that a simple statement of an earlier effort, including the stress and storm, might be of value in their interpretation and possibly clear them of a certain charge of superficiality."

Study Rationale

All historical narratives lack evidence. Intentionally or not, populations may be omitted (usually those that are marginalized to begin with), statistics may be missing, or critical archives may have been destroyed. In social work, the researcher's rationale for using historiographic methodology is to fill a gap in information, to include a particular group in the reconstruction of a certain narrative, or to explore why a specified program has never been studied or why previous studies have drawn the wrong conclusions. The rationale exists because no one has used a historical explanation, or at least this alternative line of reasoning, for the existence of a problem or social condition.

For program planners and organizational development specialists, often called on to sort out the divergent requests of agency administrators and reconcile them with the needs of front-line workers, the use of historical analysis has a particular rationale. "Historical awareness and reasoning . . . can make a customarily present-minded and future-oriented profession more effective," write Abbott and Adler (1989, p. 467). When organizations, communities, or even nations are fixated on their traditions and myths, a historical study that explores these entrenched beliefs is particularly useful. The rationale lies in the gap between "how we've always done things" and present-day demands. In 1986, Richard Neustadt and Ernest May, two professors at Harvard's Kennedy School of Government, wrote *Thinking in Time* to help their students use history when confronted by practice problems. They extracted six starting points, each of which could form a rationale for a historical study: (1) a plunge toward action, (2) overdependence on "what if" analogies, (3) inattention to or denial of an issue's own past, (4) failure to think critically about key presumptions, (5) stereotyped suppositions about people or organizations, and (6) little or no effort to see choices as part of any historical sequence (or its opposite, where history is the only justification for choices).

EXAMPLE: In their pathbreaking reinterpretation of the history of American public assistance, Piven and Cloward (1971, p. 3) state that their rationale was "not so much to describe the public welfare system (as relief-giving is known in the United States), for that has been done often enough. Rather, we seek to explain why relief arrangements exist, and why— from time to time—the relief rolls precipitously expand or contract."

Problem Formulation

The historian Carl Schorske based his vanguard book on "a problem of history: the relationship of politics and the psyche in fin-de-siècle Vienna." Why is this a historical problem? Because, Schorske says, the question that "was felt and seen by the Austrian intelligentsia . . . [was:] How had their world fallen into chaos? Was it because the individuals. . . contained in their own psyches characteristics fundamentally incompatible with the social whole? Or was it the whole as such that distorted, paralyzed and destroyed the individuals who composed it?. . . These questions are not new to humankind, but to Vienna's *fin-de-siècle* intelligentsia they became central."

A historical problem is beguiling, and formulating one requires equal parts of curiosity, imagination, and sheer perseverance. Social work is full of front-rank scholars, but historical studies have not held the stage because researchers have, so far at least, fallen short in identifying a need for investigating how our historical knowledge is constructed. How can one recognize a historical problem? Regardless of one's chosen approach, doing history means asking sharp questions and then attempting to answer them by studying the evidence. But historical research is not limited to evidence found in written documents. Sources of historical knowledge fall into three broad categories: what is written, what is said, and what is physically preserved. A good researcher consults all three data sources in order to identify a meaningful historical problem.

The same three categories of data will later be used for the in-depth investigation, but preliminary research is just as necessary in order to decide which problem the study will attempt to solve. The researcher generally starts by reading and comparing secondary sources such as monographs and journal articles. The second step is to clarify points of view that emerge from the content, including contradictions between texts. Third, the researcher locates relevant primary sources, reviews them critically, and searches out explanations within the texts. But because even primary sources are by nature subjective, the researcher also needs to refer back to secondary sources for outside interpretations that support or contradict the primary sources. A historical problem emerges when the researcher starts to question these readings. Why does a certain contradiction exist? For example, why does a social service agency continue its traditional practice method when the community it serves needs something else?

Historical problems can be found in all types of situations, both within and beyond the standard realms of activity for social workers. Asking historical questions doesn't neutralize the social problem under study, but it does demand that the researcher begin to articulate what is known about the problem, what is not clear, and, most important, what has traditionally been presumed about a situation. Clearly, the problem has to be framed correctly and within the context of the study's hypothesis. But the history writer's true challenge is not only to probe social problems from different angles but also to persuade readers that problem-posing research has something essential to offer. Whether history has predictive value, as George Santayana would have us believe, is debatable, but asking historical questions that critically examine past assumptions and expectations, does have indispensable analytical value today.

EXAMPLES: Joel Kovel (1988) describes how, "emboldened by the discovery of the forgotten radical history of psychoanalysis[,]I learned that my old ideal, Reich, had been a leading Marxist, and that Otto Fenichel, whom I had always taken for a high priest of analytic orthodoxy, had been one too. Why was this not taught?. . . Why were its implications not drawn—for if psychoanalysis had been this way once, and if its radical content had been repressed, then should there not be a recapture of that repressed truth?"

In *Sexual Politics, Sexual Communities: The Making of a Homosexual Minority in the United States 1940–1970*, John D'Emilio articulates a crucial problem in deciphering the history of the homosexual minority in the United States: "Why. . . did a gay emancipation movement come into existence only in the post–World War II era? And why did it not become a mass movement until the end of the 1960s?" (1998, p. 3).

Hypothesis Development

The methodology of historical research is largely similar to other disciplines in its regard for knowledge, its search for relevant data, and its creation of hypotheses. A good hypothesis is the forceful central concept, the core of a good study that can be tested for reliability and validity. It is a statement that clearly frames a particular historical problem that the researcher intends to resolve in the work. The hypothesis is neither the topic, a general area of inquiry, a statement of opinion, a belief, nor a thought. Instead, it is a statement that proposes to explain causal relationships between historical factors, or the causal patterns of historical change. As in systems theory, a hypothesis declares that change in one event results in another event, or a modification in the first event to which it is causally connected. Researchers usually have a hypothesis in mind when they begin their work, something they want to prove or justify. One or two sentences are sufficient to summarize the reason why one event caused another one to occur when and where it did. "The stock market crash of 1929 caused the Great Depression" is a simple hypothesis; a more comprehensive hypothesis might be "The Depression was the consequence of the unstable international banking structure of the 1920s, exemplified by the Dawes Plan of 1924." The hypothesis more or less anticipates the findings, in that the data will either confirm or disconfirm the hypothesis. Imagine using an archive like a scientist would use a chemistry lab for research to prove or disprove a causal relationship.

Hypotheses emerge from deep research, from locating reliable and credible patterns, ideas, and variables that are repeated throughout the texts. Forming hypotheses from complex data signifies the researcher's ability to gather, weigh, and sift evidence. But where the handling of source material demands care and technical competence, it is mainly in the construction of hypotheses and in the establishing of causal relationships that a researcher needs intellectual rigor. Of course, historical research can transform a simple inquiry into a philosophical quest. But a solid hypothesis gives this quest a skeletal model around which the researcher can bring to life the better part of scattered variables. Note that nothing here suggests the researcher must like the hypothesis or its testability, but the desire to logically prove (or disprove) something does enhance one's motivation and perseverance—both of which are critical to the study. The researcher should review the hypothesis periodically, not looking for an ultimate resolution but rather at how the case is being made given the initial assumptions and the characterization of the historical problem. Does the logic of the study emerge as a whole?

EXAMPLE: This is the hypothesis around which Piven and Cloward (1971) structured their ingenious study of historical patterns in welfare distribution: "Relief arrangements are ancillary to economic arrangements. Their chief function is to regulate labor, and they do that in two general ways. First, when mass unemployment leads to outbreaks of turmoil, relief programs are ordinarily initiated or expanded to absorb and control enough of the unemployed to restore order; then as turbulence subsides, the relief system contracts, expelling those who are needed to populate the labor market."

The causal relationships in this hypothesis are:

1. If American unemployment runs unusually high, then welfare expands to mitigate social upheaval.
2. If unemployment decreases, so does welfare.

3. If welfare decreases, people who have recently been unemployed will rejoin the labor market—but at lower wages.

One more note on hypotheses: many historical studies, especially those written from a postmodern perspective, may seem to be driven by a "question" or "problem" instead of a hypothesis. True, the nature of historical inquiry is more nuanced, perhaps less rigid, and more noticeably influenced by subjective interpretations (stated or unstated) than most quantitative social or behavioral science research, where statistical data analysis confirms or refutes particular assertions. Nevertheless, I propose that a researcher should start by formulating a well-crafted hypothesis to guide a study, especially if this is a doctoral student's first foray into the area.

Term Definitions

Key terms (or variables) in the hypothesis must be defined through a review of the research and theoretical literature regarding the concept. More than a glossary, creating literature-based definitions will help both author and the reader (with or without social science backgrounds) understand the terms and concepts used in a historical study. The term of interest should contain information, including the term's pronunciation if necessary, explanatory sources, even images and external links to related concepts. Both quantitative and qualitative variables can be used in the collection of historical information. A word or a concept, apart from the impressions or feelings it creates in the reader, suggests an association of larger reactions that should be developed clearly and systematically. For example, the word *apartheid* denotes a political and economic policy of segregation by race, but its connotations—oppression, slavery, inequality—are numerous. Barbara Levy Simon (1994) builds an entire historical treatise around the term *empowerment,* and she is careful to explain exactly how she intends the concept to be used. "*Empowerment* has achieved the dubious distinction of being among the tiny handful of concepts, along with *freedom, equality,* and *welfare reform,* that signify opposite meanings to political antagonists," she writes (p. 8). "To contemporary

champions of laissez-faire economics and minimal government, empowerment means handing off to people in local areas the responsibility for
making their everyday lives better. To present-day advocates of an activist
democracy. . . *empowerment* invokes the principle of subsidiarity by
which 'larger and more powerful political and economic institutions sus-
tain smaller communities instead of dominating them'. . . It is the premise
of this book that the second meaning of empowerment has been a central
philosophy of one stream of social work for approximately a century."

Presuppositions and Values

In historical research, social beliefs and personal values abound on both
sides: those carried by the researcher and those contained within the
evidence. Invariably, the biases of the information, the narrators, and
other researchers must be weighed against each other. How do the ideas
and values in the source differ from current ideas and values? Are the
researcher's initial assumptions about the work correct or not? What pre-
conceptions do readers bring to bear on this text? For instance, what
parts of the text might we find objectionable but contemporaries might
have found acceptable? Do our values on that subject contradict the
values expressed in the text? Sometimes, of course, this is a good thing:
we should be able to object to anti-Semitic statements or racism or sexism
in a text. On a more subtle level, though, the difference between our personal values and those of the author can lead us to misinterpret the text,
or to understand it in a way that the author's contemporaries would not
have (even if that understanding is offensive to us today). Ultimately,
how do history writers establish their own objectivity or come to terms
with their own subjectivity in qualitative and quantitative historical
research? Beyond verifying the facts and the credibility of claims in the
text, as well as the reliability of the source, researchers ought to follow
Marcus Robyns's (2001, p. 368) excellent guidelines:

1. Detect and determine bias both in the source of information and in
   ourselves as researchers.

2. Identify unstated assumptions.

3. Find ambiguous or equivocal claims or arguments.

4. Recognize logical inconsistencies or fallacies in a line of reasoning.

5. Distinguish between warranted and unwarranted claims.

6. Determine the strength of the argument.

EXAMPLE: Imagine that a researcher has located the 1864–65 diary of Carrie Berry, and it is pertinent to the researcher's project on the resilience of girls in wartime. From a close reading and contextual evidence, one can infer the social norms to which the 10-year-old child responded in her writings. In the early nineteenth century, female schoolteachers instructed girls in journal writing and then read their journals. How much did this influence Carrie's journals? How was she influenced by religion? By the war? Although she lived through some of Atlanta's gloomiest days of the Civil War, Carrie's images fairly explode with buoyancy. Personality aside, the researcher looks for the narrator's social and personal values within the narrator's own historical context. Reading this and other diaries requires one to ask: "How do I view what she wrote? Do I admire her character or despise it? How do I respond to the social influences I interpret in her diary?"

Data Collection Strategies

When it is finished, a historical study should read like a well-told, multifaceted story, one that attempts to give context to an event or to people without diminishing them or their contributions among their peers. As we have seen in Chapter 1, a history writer can interpret an event through one or more lenses. In turn, this interpretation leads the writer to formulate a historical problem, to develop a hypothesis, and to isolate certain variables that will serve to structure the study. The next step is the collection of data, which, once analyzed, will either uphold or rebut the hypothesis. Data collection is the systematic gathering of information and evidence. The process is separated into two major formats—quantitative and qualitative—and historical studies are apt to be colored by whichever of them the researcher uses. Most historical data and archival records are qualitative in that they consist of more words than numbers—descriptions, stories, reports, interpretations. Unlike quantitative investigations which rely on observable actions (what, where, and when), qualitative research explores how people understand or explain behavior (why and how). Numbers (days, dates, hours, money) are, of course, interspersed, and often add effective illustrations. But the tendency to obsess over bits of data and over how to organize them into a valid and reliable study reflects the equally strong tendency to feel that researchers need to choose one over the other. It also reflects the academic's desire to show that methodological consistency is as essential to a study as the data itself. Fortunately, in historical studies one is better off combining research methods and developing an evidence base that mixes quantitative and qualitative than with either one alone.

Example of Overall Design and Method

"The challenge is to find substantive ways in which to link the economic history of the interwar years with the personal and social experience of its contemporaries," writes Michael Bernstein, who took a practical approach to figuring out a definite cause of the Great Depression. In "The Great Depression as a Historical Problem" (2001), Bernstein covers the features of historical research methodology (hypothesis, purpose, rationale, problem formulation, presuppositions and values, and data collection skills). Here are the elements:

1. Hypothesis: "The Great Depression [was] the outcome of an interaction between cyclical forces dating from 1929 and tendencies of long-run development spanning a half-century or more" (p. 10).
2. Purpose: "The vast majority of contemporary economists have grown decidedly hostile to arguments concerning the Great Depression that do not focus on the short run or on policy failure. In this respect, they have avoided the structural, institutional, and long-run perspectives . . . It is for this reason that I seek, through a

reassessment of these older analytical approaches, . . . the insight
afforded by an understanding of the Depression as historical
problem" (p. 2).

3. Rationale: "It is now well over a half-century since the Great
   Depression of the 1930s, the most severe and protracted economic
   crisis in American history. To this day, there exists no general
   agreement about its causes, although there tends to be some
   consensus regarding its consequences" (p. 1).

4. Definition of terms: "The 'business confidence' thesis . . . held that
   regardless of the mechanisms that caused the collapse, the dramatic
   slide of the stock market created intensely pessimistic expectations
   in the business community. The shock to confidence was so severe
   and unexpected that a dramatic panic took hold" (p. 2).

5. Values: "The 'business confidence' thesis was subjective . . . [and]
   virtually impossible to evaluate in the light of historical evidence"
   (p. 3).

6. Data collection strategies: "Consideration of the economic history
   of the Great Depression necessarily focuses on both quantitative and
   aggregate data that tend to obscure the human dimensions of the
   event" (p. 13).

3

Preparing to Collect Historical Data

E very researcher has to grapple with two tasks when collecting historical evidence. One is the rigorous gathering and organization
of the evidence, and the other is verifying the authenticity of the information and its sources. Data collection (or acquisition) can be characterized as a strategy—a course of action for assembling data from
various sources and then enriching that data so as to create valuable
and reusable information. Like any strategy, this one must be thoroughly designed and planned, both as a study tool and as a process
that leads to a successful project. It is exceptionally important to do
solid preparatory research before going to work in archives. The first
phase of data collection has already been articulated in the study's
rationale; the second is creating a data capture instrument; the third is
plumbing the selected historical sources for information that supports
or rejects the study's hypothesis. Ultimately, the more thorough the
preparation, the more support for the last phase of the study, the critical analysis and interpretations.

Developing the Research Instrument

In historical assessment, a data-gathering instrument is valid only to the extent that it is also reliable. Using the variables (terms) in the hypothesis, specific topics are shaped into questionnaires, tables, spreadsheets, and graphs. This data-gathering instrument, also called a data capture instrument, allows the researcher to describe background, experiences, roles, and perceptions, and to reconcile data from the beginning of the study (the sources) to the end (the findings). The same instrument is used in archival and oral history research and helps establish the reliability and validity of the study. Carefully creating this instrument should be as essential to a project as the research on which it is focused.

Data capture is the process by which data are taken from real-world primary sources, and sometimes from secondary sources, and entered into a format that gives the information a clear and understandable shape. Researchers are much better off if they concentrate first on the painstaking challenge of determining the format, collecting the data, and finally entering that data directly into computer systems. The sources of primary data (especially images or rare documents) are usually digitized or scanned, and notes from secondary sources are typically just typed. In historiography, today's researchers should think of themselves as having the capacity and expertise to enter and process any type of data, typed or handwritten.

Spreadsheets and graphing software are excellent tools for organizing, representing, and comparing data that have been collected over a period of time. Graphic grids are a simple but very helpful way of organizing data. The key difference between preformatted grids and traditional narrative paragraphs is that grids help the researcher make visual associations between distinct collections of historical data that have not been connected before. In addition, grids typically support more heterogeneous collections, so they simplify the reading of complex data. At a minimum, the software-generated grids should provide details of the resource's provenance, contents, and structure. Within the instrument, each field should be designed to contain information on a particular aspect of the resource. Researchers usually design their own sets of fields for recording data. Though a degree of imagination is necessary, one wants to avoid a "patchwork" effect, because inconsistency and imprecision in the descriptions and data entry can lead one to miss data and possibly lead to non-valid interpretations.

Invariably the data-collecting vision of the researcher determines how the instrument will be designed. At the same time, the collection process forces one to justify how each source is identified and which types of data are input. Strategic data acquisition, however, should not be limited to getting the data into the data-capture instrument. It should also identify and document the sources and eventually allow the researcher to extract data from the source efficiently and effectively. For example, archives organize their documents in accordance with accepted archival principles, including the following levels: collection, record group, subgroup, series, subseries, file unit, and item. It is important to keep track of these levels and record those in the data capture instrument because (1) a reader should be able to replicate the research and (2) all these citations must be placed in the references section at the end of the study. In some cases, the number and sophistication of fields within the instrument will fall short of what the researcher had envisioned. History writers want to be practical and not feel they are wasting time on a format when so much research is waiting. But modifying or updating the instrument is sometimes necessary, and changes may be warranted even during the data collection process.

Those data capture instruments that work well for most social science research, also work well for historical research. The researcher plans the instrument as much to keep the wrong sort of data out as to put the right kind in. Consider whether or not the design meets the specific goals of the study. Once the data are collected and sorted out, will they form a foundation on which to build an answer to a historical problem? Do the categories in the instrument line up with the study's hypothesis? Finally, does the instrument realistically categorize the data so as to facilitate its analysis later on?

"How can we capture women's lives in an adequate way and what tools are available for analysis?" asks the British researcher Karen Davies (1996, p. 579). Using a feminist historiographic lens, Davies challenges the conventional data capture instrument that is structured along a chronological timeline; this kind of mechanistic social science research is problematic, Davies says, because it limits our ability to capture the intrinsic complexities of human lives in society, especially women's everyday lives. Instead she proposes that investigators should make use of a "life line" as a data capture tool in historical research. Where the traditional calendar line captures data in a solely chronological sequence, the life line shows the intersections of work time and family time, of home responsibilities and paid labor, of actions and events in relation to the individual's age. This kind of data collection reflects not only the social construction of women's relational patterns but also critical connections between the life choices women makes and the larger political situation at the time. For example, the utilization of abortion services could easily be studied along a straightforward chronological time line—but would it capture how women actually experienced abortions at various historical points (say, 1820, 1965, 1973)? A history writer who uses the life line model would instead look at what point an abortion occurred in a woman's life and how her decision—and her future development—was affected by the changing federal laws. This kind of data capture instrument opens up a range of new possibilities for social work researchers.

Example: Jeanine S., U.S. citizen, 1965

Lifeline history:				
employed	abortion	loses job	pregnant	insurance denied
Chronological history:				
abortion still illegal in most states; civil rights legislation spurs abortion rights movement				

What constitutes a historical "event"? Accounts of historical events can be divided into single events and clusters of events. A single event is, for example, Freud's 1909 visit to America, whereas a relevant cluster of events is the Progressive Era and concurrent advances in American behavioral sciences. Clusters can explain the overall context in which a single event (also called a node or nodal moment) occurred.. On a micro level, the idea of a cluster structure is to play down the impact of a single event. On a larger scale, the researcher can follow complex social and cultural themes leading up to broadly defined episodes in history such as "modernism" or "feminism."

In the 1930s and 1940s, Adolf Meyer and Sandor Rado captured the imagination of the mental health establishment in the United States with surprising force. Applying the *node-cluster model* of historiography, Craig Tomlinson (1996) used primary sources (uncited archival material, principally letters) to document how the relationship between these two men influenced American psychiatry and psychoanalysis at a fateful moment in the evolution of both. Their interaction not only framed a crucial schism within American psychoanalysis but also epitomized a historical juncture in the relationship among medicine, academic psychiatry, and psychoanalysis in North America.

Quantitative methods are relatively new to the field of social work research. Some of the most exciting recent historiographic work, however, takes advantage of computing skills that our colleagues in other areas of social science research have already mastered. At the same time, scholars are probing unpublished records and original documents without, one hopes, unduly neglecting other types of narrative sources. Quantitative data can corroborate archival and oral evidence quite effectively. To substantiate the documentary information found in archives, researchers should pursue as many data sources as possible, from eyewitness accounts for the human experience of the event to large and small-scale numerical data sets. Who is best suited to tell a particular story, an actual participant or an outside observer? While there may be some disjunction between the results of each method, ultimately it is in combining them that one arrives at a more or less truthful conclusion.

Documents: Collecting Archival Data

Facts are scattered in places all over the world, close and remote, but eventually the researcher must create something out of all the pieces. As a result, most modern history researchers make intensive use of archival institutions, largely for the purpose of retrieving and reviewing primary sources that have already been gathered in a single institution. There, significant records are identified, acquired (by donation or purchase), arranged, physically preserved, and safely secured. Archival institutions also retain the legal and physical custody of these materials. Rich lodes of data, such as the U.S. Census, economic and political surveys, genealogical materials, and public records, are already posted on the Internet. Really vibrant research takes shape on location as one peruses, reads (at times quixotically), and takes notes on documents. Not surprisingly, archival sources are also used as baseline and comparative data in studies using other research methods, particularly qualitative and oral history data.

Archival institutions are separated into *archives* and *manuscript repositories*. Many archives, such as the National Archives in the United States and the Public Archives of Canada, maintain governmental records. Private or nongovernmental archives, such as those in banks or hospitals, administer the historical records of a single institution; the archives of the Banque de France hold the records of and are part of that bank. University archives acquire historical material from faculty, administration, and students. The Manuscripts and Archives Department of the Yale University Library, for example, holds the records of the university and is a part of the university.

In contrast, manuscript repositories are archival institutions dedicated to the careful arrangement and preservation of original documents. Manuscripts are individual documents or groups of records that have historical value or significance, and include personal papers (written or typewritten), first editions, sheet music, medieval texts on vellum, and the records of non-university organizations. Sometimes called "special collections," manuscript repositories acquire, preserve, and make available archival and manuscript collections for the use of visiting scholars, researchers, and members of the public.

Much preparation is necessary—and very useful—before actually setting foot inside an archive or manuscript collection. Regardless of how familiar one is with library research techniques, archival research requires a set of different skills because of the unique way in which the materials are categorized and filed. Since archival resources are essentially unlimited, advance preparation should be strategic. Tracking down the right sources is time-consuming but crucial, and launching oneself in the right direction will ultimately save both time and anxiety. Consider taking these important steps:

- Many documentary collections publish in-house newsletters and journals: find the tables of contents of their new and old publications (both digital and printed).
- Check the bibliographies and subject indexes of secondary works for references to the exact location of primary sources.
- Check electronic and traditional (printed) bibliographies, guides, and other finding aids for archival documents; in addition to the pages for federal and regional archives and electronic databases (essential for every researcher), browse through the pages that present archival projects, recent publications, and agency news.
- Since almost all archives request that researchers contact the institution's staff before their visit to determine the availability of the materials they wish to consult, find out the protocol for access to each collection.
- Determine restrictions on access and confidentiality provisions before attempting to retrieve written documents, machine-readable records, records and audiotapes, film, and videotapes.
- Compile an individualized database of relevant and available sources.

More Planning

The Internet has doubtless become the first choice of both novice and expert scholars searching for archival sources. Traditionally, librarians have helped researchers with reference services such as genealogical research, searches for documents upon request, and compilation of topical bibliographies. Today, though, access to the Internet allows researchers to do the same work on their own, and to explore a wealth of digital media from virtually any computer. The stock of Web sites containing digital images of historical photos, archival documents in electronic form, online descriptions of archival collections, and other unique material related to archival research is expanding constantly. In one way, this technology has relieved researchers of the geographic and time inconveniences of archival work. James Schick (1990, p. 207) describes how technology is giving rise to new collegial relations and how "the relative isolation of scholars and the need for pilgrimages to document repositories may diminish as academia enters the global electronic community." In another way, however, the same technology has created a host of new potential problems: the sheer number of Web sites is overwhelming, their usefulness varies widely, and—most important—their academic reliability may be questionable. Again, this will probably change in the future as electronic research becomes more and more sophisticated, but even as I write in 2007, the relationship between computer technology and individual research remains the weakest link in original historical research.

Library-based archival collections may be governed by specific restrictions or may only be available on a selective basis; before planning a research visit, always consult the collection's staff for further information. All archives have regulations for researchers using rare book and manuscript reading rooms: again, read these policies carefully before setting out.

All archives specify which documents may be required to apply for admission to their collection. All require at least one piece of current and valid photo identification (sometimes more). For archives in the United States, a driver's license is adequate, but most international archives prefer a passport (with visa if necessary). A visa that allows the bearer to visit a foreign country is a paper or ink endorsement stamped by officials of that foreign country on a U.S. passport. Guidelines are found at http://travel.state.gov/travel/requirements and are frequently updated.

A dated letter from the researcher's supporting organization or academic institution, usually signed by the student's advisor or the institution's research director, may be mandatory. This letter informs the archive's administration that the researcher's institution is willing to vouch that the research meets the standards of academic integrity.

Access to materials is carefully regulated, and archival institutions have the authority to control how, when, and where researchers can study their archival collections. Examples of institutions' guidelines include "to order or prepare themselves copies of archival documents on the subject of their research," "within technical possibilities, and with the special permission of the archival administration, to use . . . personal computers," and "use of technical equipment containing scanning devices. . . is not permitted." Researchers may also have obligations to the archive, for example, "to furnish the required reference to the source for any archival information received that may be cited or published" (Glagoleva, 2002).

Archives are now making their holdings more accessible to the public than ever before, and new technologies mean abundant opportunities for research. However, simply having access to sources does not guarantee good-quality archival research. To make the most of a researcher's time and work both prior to and during the trip to archives, planning is essential. The success of archival research depends on both the ability to find the right sources and the ability to comprehend them fully and correctly. Tracking down a particular folder or box of material within large collections can seem daunting: it demands persistence, patience, and the motivation to sift through scores of documents. But most libraries have simplified the task with their own extensive cataloging and detailed finding aids. Best of all, archival research is highly rewarding, and it can even be fun. In archival and manuscript collections, one is returning to the original source documents from which history is written.

Protocols for Native American Archival Materials

In 1997, the Native American historian Donald Fixico observed that of the more than 30,000 books written about American Indians, roughly 90% were authored by non-Indians. This constitutes, he noted, a Western canon of Indian history. As such, these historical narratives reflect the relations of power between various groups of Native people and various groups of Europeans. What is missing is the credibility owed to native narration of native pasts. All of this might seem evident in our era of respect for diversity, but if one draws information on American presidents from the Library of Congress, one should do no less for native histories. The following is excerpted from documents developed for this purpose by the First Archivists Circle; the full text is available at www2.nau.edu/libnap-p/protocols.html.

In April 2006 a group of nineteen Native American and non–Native American archivists, librarians, museum curators, historians, and anthropologists gathered. . . to identify **best professional practices** for *culturally responsive* care and use of American Indian archival material held by non-tribal organizations. . . .

Native American communities have had extensive first-hand experience with the ways that information resources held in distant institutions can impact their quality of life, their practice of religion, and their future as a people—sometimes with disastrous consequences, sometimes to their benefit. Libraries and archives must recognize that Native American communities have primary rights for all culturally sensitive materials that are culturally affiliated with them. These rights apply to issues of collection, preservation, access, and use of or restrictions to these materials. . . .

. . . researchers [should] obtain clearance from Native American communities before accessing sensitive materials. A tribal community endorsement will strengthen the value of a research publication. In 1991, the Cline Library at Northern Arizona University and the Hopi Tribe agreed that sensitive ceremonial images would not be reproduced (or digitized for Internet access) without written permission from the Hopi Cultural Preservation Office. Access is still provided onsite. Other institutions have comparable policies; some institutions will not provide any access without prior written community authorization.

Examples of the kinds of archival materials—both human readable and digital which may be culturally sensitive from a Native American perspective include:

• Still and moving images of (photographs/ films/ graphic art) of human remains, religious or sacred objects, ceremonies of any kind, burials, funerals, archeological objects (especially from burials), hospitals, churches, cemeteries, kivas, sacred places.

• Recordings/Transcripts of songs, chants, religious practice, healing, medicine, personal or family information, oral histories, community histories, "myths," and folklore.

• Maps of sacred sites or areas, religious sites, village sites, territories, and use areas.

• Records, documents, and ephemera such as personal and family information, archeological data, religious materials, ethnobotanical materials, and genealogical data.

Interviews: Collecting Oral History Data

Mention oral history to social workers and most of them will think first of transcripts of individual or family treatment sessions. But those who do history, especially of marginalized populations, know very well the importance of cultural traditions where memoirs are spoken rather than written. "Early in my research," writes George Chauncey (1994, p. 370), "it became clear that oral histories would be the single most important source of evidence concerning the internal workings of the gay world." Oral history is a method of historical documentation that features audio- or videotaped interviews with people who experienced firsthand or were directly involved in an event and who have the knowledge and the personal desire to contribute to the record. Before World War II, interviewing fell largely to journalists and professional writers. With the advent of widespread audio- and video-recording technology, however, oral history has become accepted as a valuable historical resource. The old way of transmitting a society's experiences, through spoken stories, has been legitimized by new technologies, new methodology, and new theories.

The pioneering scholar Louis Starr defined oral history research as "primary source material obtained by recording the spoken words—generally by means of planned, tape-recorded interviews—of persons deemed to harbor hitherto unavailable information worth preserving" (Dunaway & Baum, 1984, p. 67). For example, many veterans involved in the 2004 invasion of Iraq saw the bombings of Baghdad as morally wrong, and their narratives portray a different picture of the human devastation than does the U.S. government's official story. These oral histories, and the contradictions between the two versions of the same event, may offer interesting prospects for intervention to social workers practicing in the areas of trauma, PTSD, and substance abuse. Likewise, oral history is particularly useful when it leads us to question the formal history of an event—the "official story," as it were. On the eve of the 50th anniversary of the end of World War II, Mary Palevsky, an oral historian and the daughter of one of the Manhattan Project physicists, recalled how her father's moral anguish over the creation and use of the atomic bomb clashed with his love of science. Palevsky (2002, p. 71) reviewed her father's end-of-life oral history that she had recorded, and from it realized that "what had been private questions about the bomb were part of the public debate." In turn, this questioning spurred her scholarly activism, and led her to join the controversy over the "proper" commemoration of the Hiroshima bombings.

Because of the enormous commitment of time and resources, oral history researchers will find it useful to develop a feasible plan. This plan should include a list of prospective interview candidates (along with relevant discussion topics for each), establish their relation to the historical projects, and set interviewing priorities. Describing why specific individuals are chosen to be interviewed helps the researcher prepare for the interview and improves the interview's reliability. A good oral history plan also covers background research that exposes gaps in other accounts an event. The list of subjects may change, but the very process of generating the list provides coherence and direction to the historian's overall plan. Preliminary background research begins with some simple questions such as "Has this person already been interviewed?" and "What information can I expect from this individual?" To avoid wasting time or duplicating information, obviously the researcher should decide which subjects offer the most information for the effort invested in the study.

The need for oral history has never been greater. Eyewitness accounts supplement official historical records, inform front-line social workers and leaders about their predecessors' experiences, and bringing to life museum exhibits with the words and sounds of participants. In today's media-focused world, the result is a deeper awareness and understanding of the events and human experiences that form local history and heritage.

Oral history is not without methodological flaws, of course. The problem with grounding a historical study in narrative interviews lies in its appealing (all too often deceptively so) coherent and single-toned presentation. Caution is in order, says the social historian Nicole Eustace (2003, p. 84), even though history writers should make use of human stories. "To a certain extent, narrative synthesis and theoretical analysis will always be at odds," she writes. "The fact remains that the deepest attraction of stories is their ability to create the illusion of seamless wholeness."

Two interesting subsets of oral history are *archival memories* and *indirect memories*. Certain memories remain so intact, so resistant to weakening over time, that they are "archived" in the mind. A real-world event is likely to acquire quasi-permanence—in other words, we will remember it as if it happened yesterday—if (1) it was experienced as highly emotional when it occurred, (2) subsequent events make the initial occasion feel like one of life's turning points, and (3) the event is relatively unique, not clouded by repetition. In contrast, more information than we think comes from indirect memories, from people who were not present at the event but heard about the developments described by someone else. History writers may use this kind of hearsay evidence from a "secondary witness," says Gottschalk (1969, p. 292), if they "do not rely upon them fully." To ensure some reliability, one should ask: "(1) On whose primary testimony does the secondary witness base his statements? (2) Did the secondary witness accurately report the primary testimony as a whole? (3) If not, in what details did he accurately report the primary testimony?" If the secondary witness is the researcher's only means of knowledge, satisfactory answers to the second and third questions may be construed as primary testimony. In such cases the secondary source becomes the historian's "original" or "primary" source, in the sense of being the origin of the researcher's knowledge. Just as with any primary source, the testimony of an indirect witness must be corroborated for accuracy and credibility.

Storytelling may seem unreliable at first, but respect for oral traditions comes easily to social workers who stay true to the principle of active listening. Unpredictability cannot be avoided; in fact, it should not be. And it is neither wise nor possible to ignore the profound historical damage perpetrated on indigenous groups whose stories have been decimated by conquest and genocide, or on people with intellectual disabilities who have little capacity to represent themselves. To avoid these risks, a researcher who takes human stories seriously and includes them in a historical narrative should adopt certain cautions. First of all, an interview is the recording of an individual's words voiced in response to the researcher's questions. Second, however it is recorded, the interview constitutes a formal record and must be treated and preserved accordingly. Thus oral history is fundamentally a collaborative venture that reflects the dual efforts of the interviewer and interviewee to create a unique historical source. Regardless of the particular topic, the interviewer should attempt to elicit the interviewee's thoughts and opinions as comprehensively as possible.

The careful managment of oral histories should consider the following conditions:

- *Broad conditions.* A historical tradition should be corroborated by a series of witnesses stretching from the first known reporter to the present storyteller, or to the first person who put the story in writing. Even better, several comparable and independent series of witnesses should testify to the same story.
- *Specific conditions.* Generally the tradition celebrates a significant public event, one recognized by many people who either believed in it or actively denied it, at least for a finite period of time. Garraghan (1946) suggests a limit of 150 years, at least in cultures that excel in oral remembrance. Perhaps paradoxically, the most verifiable stories include some challenge to the tradition by people who criticized it as false while it lasted. The use of narratives and storytelling by historical researchers has grown along with the importance of naturalistic inquiry in the social and behavioral sciences (Erlandson, 1993).

Narratives, folktales, and myths frame the stories people tell to evoke the core of meaning-making within their individual, family, and cultural experience. To actively listen to this narrative is to become immersed in the world of others. Interviewing community elders, for instance, allows the researcher to capture local history and the language—with its distinct words, intonations, rhythms, and imagery—of the region while at the same time empowering participants as they explore their ancestry and cultural background. This kind of evidence may seem subjective, but it is probably as close to the "truth" as any objective assessment. The self-narratives of learning-disabled children telling their stories of chaos and frustration lead Palombo (1994) to examine which metaphors reveal "personal" meanings and which "shared" meanings. For Sands (1996), a particular historical voice is heard in women's metaphors of self and identity. The voice reflects an identity constructed by intersecting layers of gender, race, class, age, and historical context.

The oral history by Maida Herman Solomon, whose pioneering career in mental health and social work practice and education spanned much of the 20th century, forms the core of a newly published primary source, *Carrying the Banner for Psychiatric Social Work: Essays, Perspectives, and Maida Solomon's Oral Memoir*. The memoir takes us back to Boston Psychopathic Hospital in 1916, then one of the country's most innovative diagnostic and treatment facilities, with vivid verbal portraits of the hospital's social milieu and Solomon's efforts to spearhead training in practice methods and community mental health.

Realia: Collecting Material Data

I am writing in my office, surrounded by technology: the laptop computer, the printer, the scanner, two telephones (one wireless, one corded). Nearby is a clock, a shredder, a lamp, an iPod, a digital camera, a surge protector. Numerous cords, power packs, batteries, cases, pens, and paper clips are tangled up in the lower left-hand drawer of my desk. In other words, I am surrounded by things. In many ways, material goods define who we are. Our lives would be unrecognizable without them, whether we actually have them available, or wish we had. When we consider material goods in historical terms we customarily see them as a measure of progress or innovation (the portable typewriter, television, the frost-free refrigerator). Cultural rituals are as much defined by the giving and receiving of material goods as they are by ceremonies. Think of wedding gifts and inherited family portraits, the intergenerational transfers of cultural artifacts. Clearly these objects, as well as their visual representations, have enormous symbolic value. Traditional ways of understanding the historical role of change in human lives have been largely predicated on our observation of tools and implements of daily life.

Realia, sometimes called *artifacts*, are found in most archival and manuscript collections, and also in the homes of oral history informants. These are physical objects, whether synthetic or naturally occurring, that do not easily fit into the neat categories of books or documents but do constitute representations of history. They include a vast array of objects such as advertising brochures, architectural blueprints, arts and entertainment programs, badges, bankbooks, bookplates, clothing, emblems and insignias, inventories, jewelry, leather goods, needlework, paintings, photograph albums, prints, postcards, posters, postage stamps, scrapbooks, wills, clothes, games, kitchen implements, furniture, draperies— all of the materials produced by human culture. Documents created specifically for a transitory purpose, such as advertisements, calling cards, notices, and tickets, are also called *ephemera*. Some individual items of historical value such as programs, posters, brochures, clippings, buttons, pennants, and stickers are also called "memorabilia."

Realia offer the researcher some of the most vivid illustrations of what has been lost and what can be recaptured. Of course, like all other forms of documentation, visual documents have to meet accepted criteria for authenticity. A photograph's provenance—the information concerning the piece's custody from its original owner(s) forward—is particularly important. This chronology may suffice for authenticating the piece, but an imaginative history writer will also want to explore what went into the visual story: the background, middle ground, and foreground details all lend a voice to the narrative. Think of the difference between a photo of someone posed with Abraham Lincoln in 1863 and a recent photo of someone posed with a cardboard cutout of Lincoln.

Numbers: Collecting Quantitative Data

Numbers count. How many Latinos voted for John Kerry in the 2004 American presidential election? How many women? How many people under age twenty-one? Analyzing these numbers can give us a glimpse of voting patterns and demographics, offering a more complete picture of the presidential race than would only archival and oral history data. This is just one example, but "all those interested in studying society, past or present, need to take charge of quantitative data: to command it rather than be a slave of a seeming authority of numbers emerging from documents or the writings of a small body of numerically inclined researchers," notes Patrick Hudson (2000, p. 17). Rich as archives are, a treasure trove of social, economic, and political data has been amassed in computerized data sets over the last few decades. Now history writers can use SPSS (Statistical Package for the Social Sciences) to present and evaluate these quantitative data in summary statistical and graphical form. The GIS (Geographical Information System) allows us to map data spatially.

Empirical historiography undeniably benefits from the use of quantitative data: they are ostensibly objective, measured with precision, detailed, accurately and unambiguously defined, and self-contained, and they lend themselves to generalizable accounts, theories, predictions, and assessments of cause and effect in the classic positivist tradition. Empirical historiography's aspirations to rigor appeal to those who repudiate postmodernism, and for whom anecdotal or oral history is interpretive, subjective, and based on value-laden data that produce non-generalizable theories and explanations. While this may be a great academic debate, in fact we recognize more and more that quantitative approaches intrinsically complement the qualitative and vice versa, especially in the description of contextual effects that are so difficult to measure.

History writers who gather and use quantitative data as historical evidence will find that numbers can be selected, set up, defined, ordered and presented in a variety of formats suited to the study. Statistical techniques can arrange and display the quantitative data so that they can be interpreted in order to answer historical questions. Even the simplest level of quantification, when applied to historical evidence, makes it possible to summarize and display large bodies of data. A table or a figure, for example, can reflect measures of average or typical experience, and can give us a powerful picture of the range of variation in a particular behavior (for example, voting patterns) over time and space. Because a clear statistical table or chart describes sets of numbers briefly and accurately, it lends itself to meaningful analysis quite efficiently. Essential descriptive statistical techniques, such as measures of central tendency and measures of dispersion, broaden our picture, and their visual presentation in graphical summaries straightforwardly complements the qualitative data. In addition to government data, researchers can start their projects by looking into the five-volume *Historical Statistics of the United States: Earliest Times to the Present* (Cambridge University Press, 2006) with its wealth of statistical data, much of it highly relevant to social welfare history.

As they develop a historical narrative, social work researchers may shy away from quantification and the use of computers in historical analysis. This is not uncommon even among professional historians. Paul Lambe, a British political scientist who has developed an entire curriculum on quantitative research methods in history, cautions that, "there is still much antipathy towards quantification by historians" (2003, p. 8). Nevertheless, when combined with other research methods, evidence gained by statistical techniques does expand our understanding of history.

4

Historical Data Sources

Historical research sources, a category whose dimensions defy measurement, date back to pre-history and are continually evolving within and across nations, and beyond. The idea of beginning to investigate these sources can evoke strong personal reactions: excitement, frustration, astonishment. Traditionalists may bemoan the advent of web-based technology and electronic data storage, particularly the use of highly configured search interfaces on the Internet. And for the contemporary researcher well-versed in the ways of cyberspace, the word "archive" does carry a slightly moldy sound. Yet for both those who are irritated by today's technology and those who carry a vehemently intellectual approach to data collection, the active investigation of primary sources redeems archival research. Effective research does require significant use of primary sources, but secondary sources will help contextualize, explicate, and defend the study's hypothesis. The sources for historical research are many and varied, and their geographic spread varies with the scope of the study: a study of a local AIDS agency can be limited to a single city or community, but an analysis of employment trends under Roosevelt's New Deal should go national. Great faceless library walls rear up like castle battlements, which at an earlier time of construction welcomed a different kind of researcher. Today's researcher is encouraged to cast the widest possible net, including Internet searches, oral history interviews, original documents, and three-dimensional objects along with archival research to make the historical study feel fresh, democratic, and inviting.

The study's hypothesis guides researchers as they decide on their prospective sources including *primary, secondary, interview subjects*, and collections of *realia*. The best project includes as wide a sampling of sources as possible—not just the oldest or best-known, but anyone and anything that helps formulate a reasoned response to the historical problem.

Primary Sources

Primary sources are by far the preferred elements in historical research. "Finding and assessing primary historical data is an exercise in detective work. It involves logic, intuition, persistence, and common sense," write Denzin and Lincoln (1998, p. 252). Modern historians favor primary sources, whether accurate or not, because they add new facts or ideas to historical questions. And they are often exciting, like archeological excavations: discovering and exploring a text allows a scholar to relive earlier events. Primary source documents add an authoritative voice to scholarly writing and allow researchers to stretch their imagination and exercise their academic creativity. As the librarian Kathleen Craver (1999, p. 8) says: "Primary sources allow students to make connections to their own ideas and develop multiple interpretations of meaning." Of course, primary sources are not just books; they can exist in oral, visual, and electronic formats. In social work, certain classic collections have taken on the value of a primary source. For instance, Robert Bremner's three-volume *Children and Youth in America: A Documentary History* is a useful selection of documents (newspaper articles, court decisions, statutes, agency reports) that illustrate developments in all aspects of the history of children in the United States between 1600 and 1970.

Primary sources of interest to social workers can be unapologetically political pieces that illustrate, for example, the horrors of sex trafficking or the trauma of incarceration. These firsthand accounts may be found in manuscripts, letters, books, diaries, court records and trial transcripts, bank documents, poems, autobiographies, and newspaper accounts of events and social movements. As mentioned earlier, these "nuts and bolts of history" are often called *archival data* when they are preserved in museums, archives, libraries, or private collections, but more and more primary sources have assumed electronic form. Each day it becomes more and more feasible to download raw historical data directly from the Internet; primary sources such as speeches, poems, movies, music, and artworks are accessible by means of a search engine. Of course some letters and memoirs of famous people may be available on a bookstore or library shelf.

The effectiveness of primary sources lies in the empathy they evoke, so that a reader responds to a historical character with a sense of shared experience, perhaps sharing a bit of their mystique. Here is Emma Goldman, the early American feminist and anarchist leader, remembering her vivid feelings on listening to Sigmund Freud in Vienna in 1896. "His simplicity and earnestness and the brilliance of his mind combined to give one the feeling of being led out of a dark cellar into broad daylight. For the first time I grasped the full significance of sex repression and its effect on human thought and action. He helped me to understand myself, my own needs."

Primary sources often have a literary quality. When writing about the Nazi era, for instance, a whole body of literature was influenced by or written about the Holocaust of World War II. Such literature includes true stories of survival in concentration camps, escape, and life after the war, as well as fictional works and poetry. Examples include Saul Bellow's *Mr. Sammler's Planet*, William Styron's *Sophie's Choice*, and Art Spiegelman's *Maus*.

Traditionally, the primary source has been the gold standard of historical research, the one place where a historical fact is virtually unquestioned. But this view is changing: "No matter how it is described, no piece of evidence can be used in the state in which it is found," write Barzun and Graff (1992, p. 155). "It must undergo the action of the researcher's mind known

Emma Goldman

as the critical method." In other words, the researcher should study not only the text but also the subtext of primary documents. Primary sources should be evaluated for external validity. Here archivists are the researcher's best scholarly colleagues, as they do much of this work already in the process of determining a record's provenance and authenticity in order to classify it. Also, the content of the primary source is reviewed for its internal reliability. How credible are the statements? How competent are the authors? What are their biases? All of this speaks to the need for critical thinking skills when evaluating data from primary sources. The merit of a historical study is often judged on the author's use of these primary materials.

Note that realia are also primary sources. Researchers often appreciate the authenticity of realia for their evocative connections to historic subjects, rather than for the object's intrinsic worth, artistic merit, historical significance, or scientific value (Olson, 2001). However, most government or institutional archives are very selective and tend to reject gifts of nondocumentary objects unless they have a specific documentary value or inherently belong in the collection. For example, vaudeville sheet music fits neatly in the Library of Congress's Library of Performing Arts, or a pair of Sigmund Freud's eyeglasses would be welcomed by the museums in London and Vienna devoted to Freud. If archives do accept a large bequest of mixed objects, they generally require the donors to sign legal documents giving the archive permission to destroy, exchange, sell, or dispose of objects that, according to their best judgment, are neither manuscripts (such as typescripts or printouts) nor directly valuable for understanding manuscripts.

Diaries, autobiographies, **and** *memoirs* are an individual's personal written records of daily events and thoughts. These personal papers are created and maintained by a living individual or a family, and often include relevant news clippings, personal financial records, photographs and notes. As private documents, diaries are supposedly not intended for a wide audience but some, such as those of Samuel Pepys and *The Diary of Anne Frank,* are still celebrated on many levels: for their high literary quality, for their power to evoke emotional responses in the reader, and for their description of certain intangible qualities of a historical era. Memoirs are another autobiographical form of writing. But the memoir is different from the autobiography because it does not center on the author's own life and experiences. Instead, memoirs give an author's personal impressions of significant figures or events.

EXAMPLES: At the Minnesota Historical Society, the diaries in the Lydia Paulson Papers reveal the work, family, and social life of a female laborer in Minnesota from 1922 to 1975. The Harry L. Hopkins Papers at Georgetown University's Lauinger Library include diaries by Franklin Delano Roosevelt's most trusted advisor covering the period 1932 to 1946. Diaries recording the experience of Julia C. Stimson as head of the Army Nurses Corp in World War I can be found at the New York–Presbyterian/ Weill Cornell Medical Archives. And a draft version of Frederick Douglass's autobiography, *Life and Times of Frederick Douglass,* and a diary kept by Douglass during his tour of Europe and Africa in 1886 and 1887—the only known documentation for certain periods of his life—are in the Manuscript Division of the Library of Congress.

Data files, such as census statistics or agency budgets, also count as primary sources if they have been tabulated but do not include commentary. Data files have generally been transferred from their original format to a machine-readable form or may exist only as electronic resources. To best use these data, the researcher should have basic knowledge of statistical methods and statistical computer packages.

EXAMPLE: The Current Population Surveys, computer files distributed by the Interuniversity Consortium for Political and Social Research, are not government documents but regularly provide the government with baseline information for making population projections, analyzing poverty and unemployment, and studying demographic trends.

Government documents can be invaluable sources. In 1934, the U.S. government established the National Archives to house its retired records; the Federal Records Act of 1950 authorized the establishment of intermediate records repositories in regions designated by the General Services Administration. Today, each of the states has its own independent archival agency. The provenance, rather than the format, makes government information unique. Whether in print or online, government publications are created or compiled by employees of a government agency, at government expense, or as required by law. Federal, state, and local government agencies continually update their information products, all of which are publicly accessible (though certain papers and correspondence generated within government offices may be considered not public information but part of the agency's records or archives). The format may be a Web page, a book or monograph, a report, a map, or a machine-readable data file. Interestingly, some papers and correspondence generated within government offices are not "published" or easily accessed by the public: these are considered part of the agency's records or archives.

EXAMPLES: The Community Services Administration created files to track grants made to local community action programs and social welfare organizations. These files are available at the Electronic and Special Media Records Services Division (NWME) of the National Archives at College Park, Maryland. The Minnesota Historical Society houses government documents detailing the state's efforts to encourage immigration from 1867 through the 1920s. The Lehman Social Sciences Library at

Columbia University has been a depository for U.S. federal documents since 1882. And papers of the Supreme Court, U.S. attorneys general, solicitors general, and appeals court judges on key court cases regarding the administration of labor law can be found in the Library of Congress.

Running records are documents such as annual reports and case records made, received, or maintained by private or nonprofit organizations (government agency, church, business, university). An organization's records typically include copies of letters, memoranda, accounts, special reports, photographs, as well as incoming letters, reports received, and memoranda from other offices. These records may contain enormous amounts of information. While charts, graphs, and tables can seem bland at first, the combination of stark rows of numbers and often sophisticated demography, can make even the most austere-looking data a researcher's treat. Running records are especially worthwhile for investigating the history of hospitals, regulatory agencies, and child welfare or other social service providers.

EXAMPLES: The Rockefeller Foundation Archives held by the Rockefeller Archive Center in Pocantico Hills, N.Y., record the life cycle of grants from initial inquiries to conclusion and include correspondence, institutional minutes, internal reports, publications, officer diary excerpts, and foundation grant actions. The New-York Historical Society houses records of the Ladies' Christian Union, an organization that provided affordable housing to young women working and studying in New York City starting in the mid-19th century. Nearly every progressive group active between 1922 and 1941 is represented among the records of the American Fund for Public Service, which are located at the American Fund for Public Service Records 1922–1941, Humanities and Social Sciences Library, New York Public Library and include internal and external correspondence, meeting minutes, committee reports, and surveys.

Serials, or serial publications such as magazines and newspapers, are incredibly valuable primary sources because they publish immediate and usually quite vivid accounts of (and reactions to) historical events. The American periodical press is almost as old as the earliest colonies themselves. Since then, serial publications have played a continual and important role in the intellectual and social life of national and local communities. Bulletins, newsletters, professional and trade journals, and other serials have served the needs of history writers, in that they have recorded the breaking news of many individual discoveries and organizational actions. To use serials as primary sources, the researcher should first identify what publications existed at the time and place under consideration. Fortunately, many serials have available indexes. Because of newspapers' frequent publication and extensive coverage, and because of the sheer number of (fairly short) articles in each issue, few produced a printed index. The two exceptions—the *New York Times* index (1851 to the present day) and *Palmer's Index to the Times of London* and its successor, beginning in 1790 and continuing till today)—illustrate history with an immediacy rarely found elsewhere except perhaps on a newspaper's Web site. Nevertheless, one may spend hours poring over issue after issue, or scanning reel after reel of microfilm, searching for the mention of an event or a person. Periodicals, in contrast, are indexed often and thoroughly: most journals append an annual index, and independent periodical indexes aggregate hundreds of same-subject entries by author and by subject. Such indexes have expanded vastly with the development of the Internet.

When serials have archival status, libraries generally control access just as they do to other collections. Here, for example, is the policy of the University of Chicago Library, from its Web site (www.lib.uchicago.edu/e/spcl/archser.html): "All serials in the University Archives are available for consultation by bona fide researchers. Some of the most heavily used serials are available to the public in the Archival reference section on the first floor of Special Collections . . . All other serials are available at the Special Collections circulation desk upon submission of a call slip indicating the title and issues desired. Additional copies of some serial titles are also maintained as part of the General collections of the Library. Serials and other University publications may sometimes be found in archival records of particular University offices or departments, and in collections of papers of faculty members; consult the finding aids to individual archival collections, available onsite in the Special Collections Research Center and online."

EXAMPLES: The American Radicalism Collection at the Michigan State University Libraries contains serial publications of leftist political parties and racist and neo-Nazi organizations along with advocacy and social change publications. There are also strong holdings of underground newspapers from the 1960s and 1970s. An index to the *Cherokee Phoenix*, the first newspaper issued by an American Indian nation, itemizes the published laws and public documents of the Cherokee nation, relevant news of the day, and miscellaneous information calculated to lead the Cherokees toward "civilization." This index can be found at the Sequoyah Research Center at the University of Arkansas at Little Rock.

The New-York Historical Society newspaper collection includes original colonial New York papers, other newspapers published prior to 1820, commercial and political dailies, and most of the principal newspapers of the northern and southern cities up to and through the Civil War.

Using Archival Materials

In a researcher's mind, a document may be simply what its title states—for example, the annual report of the Northern Dispensary for 1876. For the original author(s), though, the document may very well have had other meanings. So researchers need to train themselves to understand documents correctly.

On-site reading of archival materials can be taxing even for veteran scholars. The ink may have faded on a handwritten document, or the paper may be fragile and in poor physical condition—charming at first view, but onerous in the long run. An author's handwriting may be difficult to decipher. Even typewritten texts can be tricky if the ink has smeared or discolored. Newspapers and journals vary in quality but tend to become brittle over time.

Most archival institutions seek to preserve their original documents and for that reason will give researchers facsimiles or microfilms to review. This does not automatically ease reading, as the quality of these media varies. Before the vast expansion of digital technologies in the 1990s, microfilm was the preferred practical medium for copying records to protect against risk, as preservation against normal deterioration or damage, for use in international exchange, in lieu of direct loan or as a convenience to scholars, and for reducing costs of repair, binding, and storage. Microfilm roll film is just one of any of a number of generic products and processes (called microforms) making use of greatly reduced images that require magnification to read. Others include microfiche, microfilm jackets, and microcards. Though this is changing, today more records (especially of newspapers and periodicals) are still to be had on microfilm than in digital form.

Different terms are used to describe methods for reading archival materials, but they are generally divided into two groups, graphical and logical. The *graphical* method applies to research with handwritten documents, and calls for knowledge of (or research into) the standard handwriting of a historical period. For example, the 18th-century scholar's penmanship is different from the 20th-century professor's, and the handwriting of a first-grader of any era will be far removed from that of an educated adult. Handwriting samples (and their printed versions) of original documents are available in reproduction, and consulting them in advance is worthwhile. For example, Glagoleva, *Newsnet: News of the American Association for the Advancement of Slavic Studies* (2002), contains a variety of samples of modern Russian handwriting along with printed versions useful for reading practice.

The *logical* method relies primarily on information about the document—its type, its date of creation, the social class of the author—and is a sort of deductive deciphering. By type of document, I mean an agency's statistical reports and intake registers, or personal letters and draft manuscripts by a social work pioneer. The type of document is relevant because official documents have an explicit structure and draw on administrative phrasing that has changed remarkably little over time. Reading an agency's recent annual report can provide a sort of blueprint for deciphering a parallel handwritten archival document. Personal papers, on the other hand, rarely follow preconditions or standards, but they do share some widespread structural elements and language informed by culture, level of education, and social class. For example, official letters tend to have similar greetings and endings whereas letters between friends vary extensively.

Careful examination of those patterns will help in the analysis of handwritten documents. One note of caution, as Patrick Hudson writes (2000, p. 7): "Personal papers and official records leave the historian with more information on the elites than on the working classes, on adult males than on women and children, on settled natives rather than on migrant or ethnic minorities, and on political and social activists rather than on the more passive majority of the population."

Photocopies of documents are often provided (though generally at a cost), and many archives now offer to scan images or provide text files (also at a cost to the researcher). The librarian will decide if documents from books and manuscripts can be photocopied by researchers themselves or if, for the sake of preservation, the duplication must be done by in-house technicians. Copying is limited to materials in sound physical condition and not subject to legal or donor restrictions. Copies are provided in accordance with the United States copyright law, are subject to curatorial approval, and are intended solely for the use of the individual submitting the request. Permission to copy a document, or to have a document copied by library staff, does not convey the right to reproduce or publish the material. For example, the University of Chicago Library specifies on its Web site (mentioned above), "The Archives will accept applications for the photoduplication of any serial unless the physical condition of the material precludes photocopying. Applications and information on procedures are available at the Special Collections Research Center circulation desk." Requests for copies of archival and manuscript materials require a specific library application form, often with a signed agreement that no document or substantial portion of a document in excess of fair use, as defined by copyright law, will be published or reproduced without the permission of the copyright holder and the library.

Special Terms Used in Archives

Before starting a project with archives or manuscripts, researchers should familiarize themselves with the following special terms and definitions.

Access (open and restricted). The availability of, or permission to use, documents held in archival and manuscript collections. Access is carefully regulated, and some records are restricted. The term "restricted access" refers to the limitations set on the use of private documents or items containing potentially confidential information, such as patient records with names, or national security data protected by law from public disclosure. In other words, some records are not open to public examination because they are deemed to contain information that might damage individual privacy or compromise public activities if disclosed. "Conditional exemptions" require the archive's administration to weigh the public's right to know against an individual's privacy rights. "Unconditional exemptions" derive from specific statutory instructions that forbid the administration to release or disclose specific records or information to the public. Restrictions may have expiration dates, after which the documents can be read by anyone or perhaps limited to particular people or classes of people. These restrictions are enforced by the archives or manuscript repository, but they may be imposed by law, by the archives or manuscript repositories that hold custody of the records, by administrative or government officials, or by donors. In contrast, the Freedom of Information Act of 1966 protects the public's rights to access information on the operation of federal agencies. For example, to obtain access to the Rockefeller Archive Center, the researcher must provide in writing a brief description of the research project, the names of individuals and institutions that are central to the study, the years covered by the study, and any geographic restrictions on the study. A staff member will respond with a description of the scope and content of relevant materials in the collections and schedule an appointment. On the researcher's first visit, the archivist will conduct a registration interview and orientation to the center's facilities, rules, and regulations.

Most institutional records in the New York–Presbyterian/Weill Cornell archives are not available for public research until 25 years after their date of creation; access to patient medical records is limited and is subject to the provisions of the federal government's privacy rule that stems from the Health Insurance Portability and Accountability Act of 1996.

The archive at the Colorado River Indian Tribe Library is accessible to tribal members; application is required by nonmembers, who must agree to abide by the rules governing the use of manuscripts. All clinical records in the Viola W. Bernard's Papers at Columbia University are permanently restricted, and many are closed for a specified period; access after the closure period will be regulated.

Collection. A collection is defined as a group of documents deliberately assembled from various sources and designed to showcase a historic era or social movement, a person's life and work, or a collector's interest. This group of documents is brought together on the basis of some common characteristic (e.g., means of acquisition, creator, subject, language, medium, form, or collector) without regard to the origin of the documents. Collections are often formed by a private individual or organization.

EXAMPLES: The Swarthmore College Peace Collection is based on a mission to gather, preserve, and make accessible material that documents nongovernmental efforts for nonviolent social change, disarmament, and conflict resolution between peoples and nations.

The Social Work Library Agency Collection, Columbia University, systematically collected social service agency records and ephemera in the form of general and annual reports, conference and workshop proceedings, position papers, and training and case documents; subjects include social work, social service, families and children, day care, aging, health and mental health, alcoholism and drug addiction, and social and physical rehabilitation.

The Jean-Nickolaus Tretter Collection in Gay, Lesbian, Bisexual and Transgender Studies at the University of Minnesota, international in scope and covering all time periods in a wide variety of media, started as the personal collection of an activist and provides a historic record of gay, lesbian, bisexual, and transgender thought, knowledge, and culture.

The Center for New Deal Studies at the Roosevelt University Library contains materials on the Roosevelts, the New Deal, and the social, economic, political, and cultural history of the New Deal era in American history, including books, photographs, videotapes, oral histories, manuscript collections, and thousands of pieces of ephemera.

Container list. This is a written listing of materials included in each container and is developed to facilitate document retrieval. A container list normally consists of the title of the series or file, the portion of the file contained in each container, and the inclusive dates of the materials contained therein. A container list may also include shelf locations. A container is also called a "box" or an "archive storage box." Regardless of the name, these are special cardboard storage containers made from acid-free materials and designed to accommodate archival materials.

Examples: The collection of materials relating to the National Urban League from 1918 to 1986 at the Library of Congress is organized by department: administrative and public affairs, community development, economic development, executive office, national committee on household employment, personal papers, and research.

The Jane Addams Papers 1904–1960, in the Sophia Smith Collection at Smith College consists of two boxes of papers and articles, including biographical information (articles, obituaries, memorials), typescripts of radio broadcasts about her, organizational and historical information about the Women's International League for Peace and Freedom, speeches by Addams, articles and printed material regarding Hull House, and a few photographs and pictures of Addams and Hull House.

Document. A document is a single item of recorded information, usually on paper but possibly also on other physical media (clay tablets, papyrus, wood, parchment, paper, film, computer tape, laser disks) made by either manual or mechanical means (such as a pen on paper or an electrical impulse on computer tape).

Examples: In the Samuel J. May Anti-Slavery Collection at Cornell University is an 1860 essay, "Is Slavery Sanctioned by the Bible?" that was awarded $100 for being the "best tract on the teachings of the Bible respecting Slavery" in the Church Anti-Slavery Society essay contest. The American Medical Association's archives contain nearly seventy years of activity by the AMA's Department of Investigation on medical quackery.

The Joseph Allred Papers in the 1819–1864. Manuscripts Department, University of North Carolina at Chapel Hill contain an August 29, 1857, letter from Vilet Lester to a former owner that chronicles her sale and change of owners since leaving; in her efforts to locate her daughter, Lester gives voice to the feelings resulting from the forced separation of her family.

Finding aid or register. Like a map or a diagram, a finding aid is a written listing that describes the scope, contents, nature, and arrangement of documentary materials within a specific collection. Basic finding aids (published or unpublished, manual or electronic) include local, regional, or national descriptive databases; guides to and inventories of collections; shelf and container lists; and indexes. Archive and manuscript repositories produce their finding aids both to establish physical or intellectual control over their records and archival materials and to facilitate the investigator's preparation for research.

The Dunn-Landry Family Papers at the Amistad Research Center, Tulane University, document the leadership of a prominent Louisiana family involved in local and national civil rights and community issues. A finding aid for this collection can be found at www.tulane.edu/~amistad/_pdfs/findingaid-landry.pdf. The finding aid for the Florence Kelley Collection, papers relating to the social worker, reformer, lawyer, suffragist, and socialist, including her residency at Hull House and the formation of Chicago labor movement, is at www.uic.edu/depts/lib/specialcoll/services/rjd/findingaids/FKelleyf.html. To find materials related to Native American organizations and Wisconsin treaty rights in the Jack D. Filipiak Collection at the Sequoyah Research Center, University of Arkansas at Little Rock, researchers can consult the finding aid at http://anpa.ualr.edu/finding_aids/filipiak.htm.

Cubic feet (or cubic meters), linear feet (or linear meters). The volume of space occupied by archival materials is measured in cubic feet (a volume one foot high, one foot wide, and one foot deep) or a metric volume measure. This measurement gives the researcher a grasp of the extent of the collection. An archives or records storage box is the equivalent of one cubic foot. Linear feet (or meters) is the measurement of the amount of shelf space occupied by archival materials within a specific collection, or the length of drawers in vertical files or the thickness of horizontally filed materials. Fifteen linear inches of letter-size files will fill an archives or records storage box.

EXAMPLES: The small American Veterans for Peace Records collection in The Tamiment Library & Robert F. Wagner Labor Archives at New York University measures 0.5 linear feet and documents work to oppose militarism and support improved Soviet relations and a progressive social agenda.

The collection of National Association of Social Workers Illinois chapter records from 1921 to 1978 at the Research Center, Chicago Historical Society is 10 linear feet; topics include founding of the chapter in 1924, the professionalization of social work, standards and ethics of social workers, codes of conduct for welfare agencies, employment practices and personnel regulations, welfare legislation, public aid matters, and changing conditions during the Great Depression and during and after World War II. At the University of Maryland, the archives of the Cuba Company, an American firm that developed railroads and sugar plantations in eastern Cuba following the Spanish-American War and substantially influenced Cuban society, politics, and economics, measure 273.50 linear feet; of particular interest in these extensive administrative records are letters in the correspondence series relating to the Negro protest of 1912 and labor disputes and strikes.

Personal papers. Personal papers collections include private and public documents accumulated by individuals or families and subject to their disposition. Personal papers usually have an organic unity, formed naturally over the course of a person's life. This group of documents shares a common underlying identity, but is generally not as complete as a collection.

EXAMPLES: The Elizabeth Prince Rice Papers in The Arthur and Elizabeth Schlesinger Library on the History of Women in America, at the Radcliffe Institute document the development of social service departments in hospitals and social work techniques for physicians.

The Martin Luther King, Jr. Center for Nonviolent Social Change, Inc., The King Center. holds the personal papers of Dr. Martin Luther King Jr. and other notable civil rights individuals. The papers of Arthur Dunham, a social worker in Massachusetts and Pennsylvania, a professor of community organization at the University of Michigan, and a pacifist imprisoned as a conscientious objector during World War I, can be found at the Bentley Historical Library of the University of Michigan.

Provenance. Provenance is defined as information concerning the original ownership and custody, as well as transfers of custody, of particular archival records. Papers and other items of Sigmund Freud were given to the Manuscript Division of the Library of Congress by the Sigmund Freud Archives between 1952 and 2001; additional material was given to the library between 1970 and 1976 by Anna Freud, who subsequently bequeathed to the library the remainder of her father's papers in her possession at the time of her death in 1982. Numerous other donors gave Freud-related material directly to the Library of Congress between 1942 and 2001, and further items were acquired by the library through purchase, transfer, and exchange between 1943 and 1999.

EXAMPLES: Material relating to Ethel Sturges Dummer was gifted to the Radcliffe Institute by Katharine Dummer Fisher, Marion Dummer Abbott, and Frances Dummer Logan Merriam in 1960, 1972, 1975 and 1976. Microfilm was purchased from General Microfilm in 1977. Additional gifts were made by Katharine Fisher, Walter T. Fisher, and the Winnetka League of Women voters between 1960 and 1963 and by Louise Young in 1980. The complete contents of the Angela Davis Legal Defense Collection was a gift directly from Davis to the Schomburg Center for Research in Black Culture at the New York Public Library in December 1990.

Record. Any information, regardless of physical form or characteristics, made or received and maintained by an organization or institution is considered a record. (The Federal Records Act definition of records can be found at 44 USC Sec. 3301.) All records are documents, but not all documents are records; the difference is that documents can be found outside an organization or institution. For storage purposes, special cardboard cartons are designed to hold approximately one cubic foot of records and to fit on specially configured industrial metal shelving.

EXAMPLES: Examples of records include baptismal and marriage records of a parish church, minutes of a town hall meeting, or Foreign Office correspondence. The records of the Brotherhood of Sleeping Car Porters 1920–1968, Manuscript Division, Library of Congress; the records of the Welfare Federation of the Los Angeles Area from 1925 to 1962 are found in the California Social Welfare Archive at the University of Southern California.

Series. An organized body of archival documents arranged according to a unified filing system, or maintained as a unit usually because they share the same provenance, function, or activity or have a particular form, is called a series.

The Equal Rights Amendment Campaign Archives Program Records at 1970—1985, Sophia Smith Collection, Smith College begins with Series I, ERACAP Administration (1981–85), and then is organized by date, beginning with 1970 and concluding with Series IV, ERA Defeat (1982–84), and Series V, Audiovisual Materials (1978–82). The materials relating to the community activist Benjamin Feldman are arranged in the Samuel L. Paley Library Urban Archives, at Temple University. Dedicated community activist archives are arranged in twelve series: Correspondence, Finances, Presentations, Consumer Groups, Group Law, Philadelphia Consumer Services Cooperative, Inc., Weaver's Way Cooperative Association, Consumer Education, Government Agencies, Organizations, Publications, and Miscellaneous.

Archive reading room protocol. The reading room of an archive is reserved for registered users, including visiting researchers. Many of the holdings are rare or unique, and readers are expected to treat all materials with care. Observance of archival protocol is fairly straightforward and can prevent possible misunderstanding and conflicts with archival administration.

Manuscript Reading Room (1990). Photo Courtesy Manuscript Division, Library of Congress.

All researchers who request access to an archival or manuscript collection must complete and sign a designated application form. Permission for access is granted on a case-by-case basis and subject to restrictions defined by federal and state law, the library's own administrative policies, gift and bequest agreements, and preservation standards. Once accepted, researchers consult the archival and manuscript materials only in designated Library "reading room" areas. Researchers must comply with stated policies for the use of rare, archival, and manuscript materials in the reading room. To avoid loss or damage, most reading rooms ask users to follow certain common guidelines:

- Cell phones, pagers, and other messaging devices must be silenced.
- Not permitted in reading rooms are food and drink, headphones, music players, recording devices, briefcases, backpacks, handbags, computer cases, coats, and hats. Free lockers for personal items are usually provided by the archive and are located inside or very near the work areas. All personal items should be deposited in the locker, except your library card, your locker key, and the permitted items.
- Only materials needed for research may be taken into reading rooms: library materials, notebooks, laptop computers, books, and digital cameras. All of these are subject to inspection prior to entering and upon leaving the reading room.
- Books, manuscripts, and archival documents may be used only in the reading room.
- All written notes are to be taken in pencil on paper (usually provided) or on a laptop or other computing device. Marking, erasing, or altering archival materials is prohibited.
- Reproduction or imaging (e.g., photography or scanning) of materials by researchers in the reading room is permitted selectively.
- All materials must remain on the surface of the table at all times. Researchers may be asked to place books and bound manuscripts on book rests or cradles, to use weights for holding books open, or to wear protective gloves. The reading room staff will inform researchers when and if this is required.

- Manuscript and archival materials are delivered to researchers one box or folder at a time.
- Only one folder should be removed from a box at any given time. After reading and taking notes on the contents of that folder, and recording the box and folder number for future reference, the researcher should replace it in the box before removing the next folder.
- The sequential arrangement of unbound materials (papers in folders and folders in boxes) must be maintained in exactly the same order in which it was delivered.
- Unlike archival boxes, more than one bound book or printed volume may be delivered at one time. Depending on their size and condition, however, the reading room staff may limit the number of books in circulation.
- All items in the reading room must be returned at closing time. Most archives will place items on short-term hold for researchers.

EXAMPLE: Due to a two-year renovation at the Archives Center, National Museum of American History, Smithsonian Institution, access to the facility and research hours were adjusted temporarily; all non-Smithsonian researchers were to be escorted to the Archives Center, and researchers were required to call or write to make an appointment and to consult with a collection specialist. Upon arrival, after signing in and placing nonessential items in a locker, researchers are required to read and agree to follow the Archives Center's rules and procedures, and to watch a short video that introduces the collection and demonstrates basic handling techniques. Researchers must use a container registration form to request materials. At Wayne State University, the collections of the Walter P. Reuther Library are open to anyone engaged in serious research; researchers planning a visit are advised to contact the Reference Archivist in advance. Researchers work in the reading room or one of several audiovisual viewing rooms; some research may also be conducted by a staff member. Collection material may be photocopied by the staff, subject to restrictions and upon payment of a fee.

Secondary Sources

Secondary sources of information are written records or accounts by individuals who neither participated in nor observed the historical event that they describe. These are an excellent foundation for starting research in the history of social work, social welfare, and social science. In fact, relevant secondary sources may be the best place for becoming familiar with the historical landscape before digging into unpublished archival or other primary sources. Secondary sources often attempt to describe, explain, or investigate primary sources and can be used as a springboard for a favorable or contentious critique. Secondary sources may also analyze or restate parts of the primary sources, but the author's intent is usually to reinterpret an original argument or rearrange historical evidence in a new way. While reading the piece, one should look for the structure of the central argument or hypothesis in order to understand how it leads to a unified composition. After identifying the hypothesis, ask how the author goes about making the case for this new work. This critical assessment of secondary works can help illuminate how a planned study may either build upon or challenge a certain historical problem.

Secondary sources include dictionaries, documentaries, encyclopedias, textbooks, obituaries, biographical dictionaries, bibliographies, and books and articles that interpret or review research works. Secondary sources can be either general (*Encyclopædia Britannica*) or specific (Bell's *Biographical Dictionary of Industrialization and Imperialism, 1880–1914*). These works can be very practical because they give the researcher an overall grasp of a subject and often include bibliographic information that can be used in further research.

Most secondary sources of interest to social workers are the work of other researchers writing history, and intellectual history. Some, however, can be construed as primary if their information is unique. Film documentaries such as Barbara Kopple's *Harlan County, USA*, for example, collect a large amount of recorded material such as newspaper stories, trial transcripts, and legal reports pertaining to a historical event.

Biographies of individual historical figures are more than a chronological catalog of impersonal facts such as birth, education, work, relationships and death. To produce a good biography, the author constructs a narrative out of a variety of primary source documents, such as letters, diaries, newspaper accounts, photographs, and official records, and includes both well-known and obscure facts and anecdotes that reveal the subject's character. Descriptively austere but often rich in interpretation, a scholarly secondary source takes in the existing secondary literature and engages with its arguments and evidence.

EXAMPLES: Romanofsky's *Greenwood Encyclopedia of American Institutions: Social Service Organizations* contains short essays on the history of many national organizations in the social service field. Walter Trattner has produced the *Biographical Dictionary of Social Welfare in America*, featuring biographical essays on selected leaders in U.S. social work, and also *Social Welfare in America: An Annotated Bibliography*, an extensive listing of sources for the history of social welfare.

Another valuable resource is the complete *Proceedings of the National Conference on Social Welfare and Its Predecessors (1874–1982)*, now available online at http://quod.lib.umich.edu/n/ncosw. For over one hundred years, the National Conference was the major meeting for the social work profession. The online proceedings, a project of the University of Michigan Libraries with assistance from the University of Minnesota, has made feasible a new kind of scholarship in social work and social welfare history.

Broadcast media. Television and radio programming is usually defined as secondary source material, but broadcasts are gaining cautious acceptance as an archival primary source. They do not fit easily into established criteria for validity and reliability of historical evidence since journalism is routinely partisan. One has only to consider the subjective quality of the *New York Times* tag line: "All the news that's fit to print." Exactly who decides what is "fit to print" and why? Yet most media are "rich in history and potential" as archival materials, says Donald Godfrey (2002, p. 501) even if they are designed with a view toward commercial and entertainment ratings and are consequently full of drama, anecdote, and "dubious historical information." In other words, one should approach a broadcast program as one would any other primary source, taking care to verify the facts by tracking and documenting the information, and establishing the context in which it was delivered. The challenge is to decide whether a news report, for example, is to be taken as a primary source or a secondary source, and Bormann (1969, p. 173) has drawn up a useful distinction: "When a reporter writes of what he or she has personally observed, be it printed or broadcast, he or she becomes a primary source." But when a reporter draws on material from participants or "informed observers or sources close to the government and 'undisclosed' sources," then the report is a secondary source.

EXAMPLES: The H. K. Yuen Collection at the University of California, Berkeley, contains recorded shows from the Pacifica network and community radio, including documentaries, interviews, and live broadcasts. Most of this content is unique and not preserved elsewhere.

The Museum of Broadcast Communications in Chicago preserves more than 85,000 hours of historic and contemporary radio and television content that documents the American experience.

Arthur Ramsey was a newsreel cameraman in Oklahoma City during the 1930s, and his footage, now at the Oklahoma Historical Society, includes scenes of events and people in Oklahoma history, many with sound. The Library of Congress archives many television programs from the Public Broadcasting Service, National Educational Television, and NBC, and all moving image materials in the collection can be viewed without charge by those doing specific research leading toward a publicly available work.

Nontraditional Sources

Sometime the researcher's most audacious stroke is figuring out how to include actual human narratives in the historical study while minimizing the risk of invalidating the design. A good study requires imagination as well as insight, so that researchers' sympathy with their subject rounds out their erudition. All voices must be heard in social work,

Table 4.1 Comparing Primary and Secondary Sources on the Same Topic

Topic	Primary Source	Secondary Source
Immigration	**Records of the United States Immigration and Naturalization Service, 1919–1926, Social Welfare History Archives, University of Minnesota.** The deportation of aliens during the Palmer Raids of 1919–1920; cases of Carlo Tresca and other radicals, anarchists, and communists.	*The New Minnesotans: Stories of Immigrants and Refugees*, by Gregg Aamot (Syren, 2006)
Slavery	**Slave Letters, Rare Book, Manuscript and Special Collections Library, Duke University.** Rare and original letters by people who were enslaved in the United States.	*Slavery on Trial: Law, Abolitionism, and Print Culture*, by Jeannine Marie DeLombard (University of North Carolina Press, 2007)
Settlement Houses	Jane Addams's memoirs: *Twenty Years at Hull House*	Books about Jane Addams
American Indians	**Alamo Navajo Oral History Project, 1977–1984, Center for Southwest Research, University of New Mexico.** Interviews with people from the reservation in New Mexico discuss Navajo kinship patterns, daily lifestyles, history, and culture.	*Rethinking American Indian History*, edited by Donald Fixico (University of New Mexico Press, 1997)
Mental Health	**Oskar Diethelm Library, Institute for the History of Psychiatry.** "My Experiences in a Lunatic Asylum, by a Sane Patient" (1879) is a firsthand account of 19th-century mental institutions.	*Seeing the Insane*, by Sander Gilman (University of Nebraska Press, 1996)
Child Welfare	**University of Minnesota Libraries, Social Welfare History Archives.** Child Welfare League of America records, 1900–2003.	*The Girls Who Went Away: The Hidden History of Women Who Surrendered Children for Adoption in the Decades Before Roe v. Wade*, by Ann Fessler (Penguin, 2006)

and this includes testimonials of witness or remembrance, individual and/or group recollections, music and songs, films, photographs, and videos—broadly, oral history. Some oral history interviews may be questionable as primary sources, and the authenticity in their information should always be corroborated with other documentary evidence. Nevertheless, they add energy and cultural substance to the historical record.

Oral history. This section offers a step-by-step outline for conducting oral history research: naming of the candidates for interviews, documenting how informants are selected for interviews, sequencing, and a plan for contacting informants and conducting the interviews.

Everyone has a story to tell, but no researcher can interview everyone. And as all researchers know (or quickly learn), time and resources are especially constrained in the social sciences. So before committing time and resources to an interview, the researchers must evaluate just how significant and useful each interview will be to the study.

Doing oral history means gathering data by asking people the questions that have already been formulated in the data capture instrument. The questions will have already been organized in a logical way, either chronologically or topically. To establish common ground, the researcher starts with some straightforward questions about interviewees, perhaps their family, when and where they were born, childhood, schooling and the teenage years. Proceed chronologically and ask about early adulthood—leaving the family of origin, education, military service, and employment. What are their best and worst memories? How did their family face certain challenges? This helps the subjects situate themselves within the story.

The course of an interview cannot be predicted. The participants' personalities, the material to be discussed, and even the location of the interview can influence it. Taking notes during the interview is very helpful, though it is all too often neglected by researchers. Interview notes may be the only source of information if, for example, the tape recorder fails. Quickly jotted notes are equally useful during the interview (pointing to follow-up questions) and afterward (for organizing one's thoughts and signaling which key words or items will require verification).

- Decide who will be interviewed, by whom, and where. Select prospective interviewees according to the goals of the study, keeping in mind that generally, the wider the interviewee pool, the more valid the study. Merely conducting a large number of interviews can take a tremendous amount of time, so while conducting all the interviews oneself promotes reliability (and enormous learning), utilizing other well-prepared interviewers or collaborative interview teams can be time and cost-efficient. Consider whether the interviews will be held at informants' homes or in a public place. Some interviewees feel more comfortable in their home, while others may prefer more neutral spaces or an academic setting. While familiar surroundings can prompt reminiscences, the interview questions can evoke unwelcome glimpses of the past, possibly turning the process into an irritating scrutiny or a form of narcissistic display. In addition, if minors are the interviewees, be aware that state and local laws might require that interviews be conducted in a designated area and under supervision.
- Allow sufficient time to prepare for the tape-recorded interviews. Inadequate interviewer preparation leads to low-quality interviews. The quality of the information obtained from an interview is integrally related to the researcher's background knowledge of the subject matter. Carefully estimate the amount of time needed to conduct the interviews and to process the tapes. Allow for the unexpected, and schedule some time for delays.
- Questions that can be answered with a simple yes or no can be convenient when confirming a specific point, but they should be followed with broader questions that lead to more expansive answers. Instead of asking "Did you attend Emerson Court High School?" ask "What was your high school like?" The school's name will emerge in the answer. Open-ended questions are different from leading questions. Leading questions can subtly indicate what the researcher thinks is the correct answer and might prompt the interviewee to respond accordingly. An example of a leading question is "Do you support a balanced budget amendment to end waste and fraud in the government?" as opposed to "What do you think about a balanced budget amendment?"

- Ask one question at a time, and reach for a full answer to each question. Statements such as "I thought that X would happen" should be followed by questions to determine why the interviewee assumed that at the time. Similarly, sweeping statements such as "We always had problems with Y" should be followed by a request for a specific example. Also, during the interview, jot down the names of people and places that are mentioned, foreign words, and other words whose spelling might need to be checked. Try not to interrupt the interviewee's train of thought; ask for clarification later on.

- Pay close attention to what interviewees say; do not leave the job of listening to the tape recorder listening for you. Effective interviews are a mix of pre-sequenced questions and free-ranging dialogue, of open-ended and specific questions that allow for feelings and subjective opinions. Combining the specific question "Who was the agency director?" with a more probing open-ended one such as "What was the atmosphere of the agency like?" will provide richer answers than either one by itself. Direct questions can help interviewees to focus their answers. Use a specific frame of reference such as "during the drive to the hospital"; this gives interviewees a starting point around which to organize a response. Try to maintain a chronology for events, and ask when one action occurred in relation to another.

- Do not rush through the interview. Allow periods of silence when the interviewees may be reminiscing, choosing what information to disclose, or balancing their need for privacy with a desire to impart information. A pause may signal that interviewees are reflecting or putting a further response into words, and that new information could be lost if the researcher is too quick with the next question. Remember that informants have agreed to be interviewed, to include the researcher in a privileged circle of information.

- Memories can change over time and are subject to influence. The task of the oral historian is twofold: to determine the accuracy of the interviewee's account (for example, by asking questions that can be corroborated by other sources) and to focus the interview on topics that are less susceptible to the passage of time. While an interviewee may not remember accurately the specific time or date of an event, certain details about the event itself will be inscribed in the interviewee's memory for all time.

• Not covering everything planned for the interview is a common experience. Focus instead on the solid answers to the questions that were asked. Stay responsive, encouraging, and respectful. Too many specific questions and not enough open-ended ones, or jumping too quickly to the next question, can frustrate both interviewee and researcher. Also stay clear of marathon sessions: no interview can last much longer than two hours without fatiguing either researcher or subject. Take a break.

• Labeling and storing are the post-interview tasks. The researcher's job is not complete until the interview is analyzable and accessible to other historians. So it is critical to label the cassettes and digital storage media as soon as the interview is completed. List the names of the interviewer and interviewee, the date, the place of the interview, and the researcher's classification. Next, back up all digitally recorded interviews, either on a CD or DVD or on a separate hard drive. Specify if an interview is recorded over several cassettes or CDs: write "1 of 2" or "1/2" on a label to identify part one of a two-part interview. Use soft-tip pens to label CDs and DVDs. If the interview is taped on cassette, press in the two tabs at the top of each cassette to prevent accidental erasure of the interview through rerecording. Store the interview along with the notes from the interview in a safe and clearly designated place.

EXAMPLES: Pioneers in Housing: An Oral History Project, 1981–1996, Manuscript Division, is located in the Library of Congress and covers public housing and community planning; the collection includes interviews with officials in the Department of Housing and Urban Development and its predecessor, the Housing and Home Finance Agency, educators in urban studies, and community developers.

Behind the Veil: Documenting African American Life in the Jim Crow South Records, 1890–1997, in the Rare Book, Manuscript and Special Collections Library at Duke University, includes oral histories of African-American life during the age of legal segregation in the American South;

interviews and family photographs of black elders documents the crucial role that black churches, fraternal societies, women's clubs, and political organizations played in African American community life, the civil rights struggles in the 1960s, African American participation in desegregation within local communities, and post-1965 community activism.

The Albert Lepawsky Papers at the Center for New Deal Studies, Roosevelt University Library, include interviews with almost 150 New Dealers, contemporary magazines and publications, sheet music, and unpublished studies of the New Deal.

5

Data Analysis

Once the data have been retrieved and pondered, it is time to cull them for findings and conclusions, to advance the inquiry from the known to the unknown, and to form a cohesive narrative that will stand the test of scholarly criticism. This is often the most exciting part of the work. Crafting the authentic source materials into a meaningful, clear-eyed writing of history is in itself deeply rewarding. This is where the researcher asserts the value of the study, bears responsibility for its reliability and validity, and undertakes the challenge of answering a historical problem. This may take many revisions. As the American poet and pundit Dorothy Parker commented, "I can't write five words but that I change seven."

While standard research studies in the social and behavioral sciences make a clear distinction between data collection and data analysis, this difference may feel more awkward for historical researchers. For one thing, from the very beginning the researcher's values and presuppositions affect how the data are collected. For another, one may ask how valid inferences are when drawn from data as complex as historical records. And the way in which questions are posed to oral history informants can influence the extent and quality of information they share.

The analysis of historical data is really an interpretation, or a reinter-pretation, of obtainable materials. In doing history, researchers do not develop new data, but rather rearrange existing data according to a new hypothesis. In "Forrester Blanchard Washington and His Advocacy for African Americans in the New Deal," Frederica Barrow (2007) revisits the history of the Roosevelt administration's New Deal through the figure of Forrest Washington, an African American social worker influential in federal legislative policy of the 1930s and grassroots organizing. Barrow's postcolonial historiographic approach to archival research allows her to get beyond the conventional New Deal rhetoric of social welfare equity. In bringing to light Washington's documents that critique the unequal treatment of African Americans, Barrow de-idealizes Harry Hopkins and offers a new and valuable perspective on government from the perspec-tive of a hitherto marginalized social work pioneer.

As always, the study's hypothesis is the core of the analysis. The hypothesis is the main argument that underlies how the researcher approaches the documents, objects, numbers, and interviews that have been collected. It is the planned, central argument of a work of history, and it is put through repeated evaluations. While writing, ask the ques-tion "Is this relevant to my hypothesis?" over and over again. "Have I used the evidence to ascertain a cause-and-effect relationship? How clearly have I constructed my argument? How is the hypothesis structured into the data collection instrument? Is the reasoning valid? Does the evidence link the hypothesis to the conclusions? Have I accounted sufficiently for presuppositions, assumptions and values?" These questions may be chal-lenging, but trying to determine the answers will advance the analysis.

Organizing the Data

Chronological Versus Topical Organization

Social workers writing history for the first time may become so deeply involved in the research that they sometimes presume, erroneously, that readers will recall every detail presented earlier in the narrative and will be eager for more. What they fail to realize is that this kind of enthusiasm has to be created, and that the system they choose for putting the data into an orderly narrative will have an enormous effect on the reader.

The first such decision to make is whether to organize the study chronologically or by topic. A chronological narrative means placing the oldest events first and the most recent events last. Peter Gay's authoritative 1988 biography of Sigmund Freud starts with Freud's birth in 1856 and ends with his death in 1939. In contrast, Jane Addams (1910, p. 6) chose to arrange her reminiscences by topic. She explains why: "It has unfortunately been necessary to abandon the chronological order in favor of the topical, for during my early years at Hull House, time seemed to afford a mere framework for certain lines of activity and I have found in writing this book, that after these activities have been recorded, I can scarcely recall the scaffolding."

Contrast and Compare

Different people will remember and write about the same event in different ways, creating new narratives from evidence. Comparing several versions of the same event and then contrasting certain selected variables allows the researcher to tease out common components or attributes. To reconstruct a historical event with accuracy, weigh several writers' accounts of the event against each other, as well as their interpretations. And since historians are endlessly involved in larger, sometimes cryptic arguments with each other, or with academics from other disciplines, it is perfectly fair to develop a "contrast and compare" study that disputes a rival interpretation.

Case Studies

Like a psychobiography or even a clinical case study, a historical case study often marries chronological history with memoirs or letters from a specific time and place. Case studies explore the compelling small steps (instances of intolerance, for example, as opposed to mass violence) that can help us grasp the complexities of the past by connecting them with our lives today. One sees how a historical event can hinge on odd particulars of personality and chance, not just deliberate method. Case studies are in-depth by definition, so one case alone is often enough to transform predetermined stereotypes.

"Now's our chance to show them the stuff we're made of—that we're real men, not the grown-up children as they want us to believe," declaimed Bruce Barton in 1914. His words are among the many moving letters and speeches in Edythe Ross's classic account (1976) of Atlanta-based African Americans' "pioneer role in devising many forms of social intervention for promoting the social welfare of the group" (pp. 298, 306) To chip away at hegemonic white-black narratives of social welfare, Ross drew on a range of local 19th-century documents from members of the Freedmen's Bureau and the Georgia state legislature, E. R. Carter's 1894 *The Black Side*, and W. E. B. Du Bois's scholarship to demonstrate "the preeminence of the city as a center of black thought and black advancement." The various forms of mutual aid, child care and welfare services, employment bureaus, health centers "where the death rate was one third lower than among the white population" (p. 302), gyms, and churches "are necessary to recall in order to destroy the myth that blacks did nothing for themselves" (p. 307).

Quantitative Studies

"How do I love thee? Let me count the ways." If Elizabeth Barrett Browning could enumerate the ways in which she loved her husband in the 19th century, surely today's history writer can use quantification with equal success. Dean Simonton, an authority on quantification, is so enthusiastic about the methodology that he predicts that "future analyses of historical data may eventually become almost exclusively quantitative" (2003, p. 638). Perhaps, but even if not all future historical studies are quantitatively based, certainly the sophisticated use of numbers should be included in most studies. Most quantitative historical analyses apply the full repertoire of measurement strategies and techniques to historical data. Once coded and quantified, concrete variables can be subjected to "the same analytical tools as seen in standard correlational studies," writes

Simonton (2003, p. 620). "These tools include factor analysis, cluster analysis, multidimensional scaling, multiple regression, structural equation models, and mathematical models." One can add frequency distributions, per capita estimates, and vital rates. A social worker writing a historical study of an economic policy might want to use economic variables such as the size of the labor force, unemployment, per capita income, and the distribution of wealth. A longitudinal study of life course and intergenerational behavior would look at demographic rates (rates of birth, death, marriage, and migration).

The reasons for using U.S. Census data as a source of evidence in historical inquiry are well established, given the present and escalating appeal of statistical information, interest in social groups, and sensitivity to international and regional comparisons. Scholars tend to trust the data because we know who collected it and why, and which scientists scrutinized these large databases for internal consistency. The wide range of available information and its richness relative to most historical sources are definite advantages. Be aware, however, that when the census is tested for internal consistency, it "may reveal certain types of misreporting or mistabulation error," writes the economist Richard Steckel (1991, p. 590), who also says that "the poor, the unskilled, ethnic minorities, the very young, residents of large cities, and residents of frontier areas are more likely to be uncounted" (p. 581). Social workers will not be surprised to find out that the least reliable quantitative information is that on the very populations for whom our studies should be promoting social and economic justice. Among the challenges that lead to omissions and misreporting are fears of confidentiality (particularly among immigrant groups), inaccessible places of residence (homeless people, for example), and lack of literacy.

Critical Evaluation of the Evidence

No matter how comprehensive one's interviews and how persuasive one's argument, historical evidence can be missing, biased, or unrepresentative. How reliable is human memory? How valid is a particular narrative?

Virtually all recorded facts rely on the judgments of individual transcrib-
ers and cannot simply be subjected to statistical verification. Most historical materials are qualitative and fragmentary and thus vary in degree
of reliability. Notwithstanding the virtually endless range of historical
topics, chances are that a great many more exist for which we have no
record, and therefore no resolution to the problems they pose. To produce a historical analysis that is accurate to the extent possible, the
researcher should combine strategies, examining both eyewitness
accounts as well as the secondary versions produced from these records.
Mixing methods and approaches has the added advantage of decreasing
systematic bias and problematic assumptions. Even for "the skeptical
qualitative historian," says Gidon Cohen (2002, p. 167), "the problems of
missing data, bias, and lack of a representative sample should not prevent
quantitative analysis. Qualitative and quantitative approaches can be
usefully combined, potentially opening up a new range of sources for
examination."

Think first and foremost about the study's central argument. After
the data have been analyzed, will the reader be able to trace the logic
of the argument? The reader should be able to answer the following
questions:

- What is the historical problem?
- What are the premises underlying it?
- What is the hypothesis?
- What points has the author developed to confirm, or disconfirm, the
  hypothesis?
- What are the author's assumptions? Have they been addressed or not?

Researchers should challenge themselves as authors by selecting one
aspect of the hypothesis and determining what primary source evidence
supports—or challenges—the their argument. Go back to the primary
source itself. Does it corroborate the researcher's interpretation?

While one aspect of archivists' mandate is to ascertain a collection's
provenance, verifying and authenticating the material evidence that the
researcher will use, it is ultimately the researcher's responsibility to assess

the reliability of the sources used in the study, with regard to their authorship, the author's expertise and credibility, and the authenticity (or corruption) of the text itself. Judd, Smith, and Kidder (1991) condone the use of public documents and mass communications because of their strong external validity, but they warn against "certain problems of interpretation, centering on internal and construct validity." Consequently, "checks against alternative sources of data and alternative explanations of data patterns should be built into the research plan." Researchers should not expect documents (or very few) to be completely reliable. Louis Gottschalk (1950), who outlined many of the classical guidelines still in use today, wrote that "for each particular of a document the process of establishing credibility should be undertaken separately regardless of the general credibility of the author." When mining a document for evidence, the researcher weighs each piece individually in order to assess the probability of an author's trustworthiness—and to protect against false evidence.

Archivists may have already done the following work, but researchers will find that repeating (or at least confirming) it will enhance their analysis and help them relate the documentary evidence back to their hypotheses. These seven questions were originally formulated by Garraghan (1946, p. 168) and are still used today to analyze the external validity of a data source:

1. *When* was the source, written or unwritten, produced (date)?
2. *Where* was it produced (localization)?
3. *By whom* was it produced (authorship)?
4. *Why* was it produced (context)?
5. *From what preexisting material* was it produced (analysis)?
6. *In what original form* was it produced (integrity)?
7. *What is the evidential value* of its contents (credibility)?

EXAMPLE: In the course of research on migration patterns of African American people from the South toward Chicago, the researcher peruses an exhibit at the Library of Congress, The African-American Mosaic, and finds an original letter written in ink on paper from Mrs. J. H. Adams of

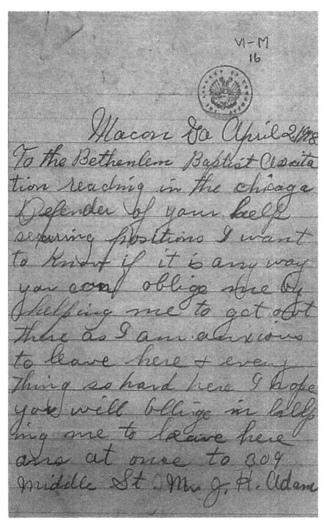

Mrs. J. H. Adams' Letter to the Bethlehem Baptist Association

309 Middle Street in Macon, Georgia, to the Bethlehem Baptist
Association, dated April 2, 1918; the letter discusses, among other things,
"reading in the *Chicago Defender* of your help securing positions." These
data answer the seven questions designed to assess external validity. The
archivist's notes that accompany Mrs. Adams' letter read: "The *Chicago*

Defender was remarkably successful in encouraging blacks to migrate from the South to Chicago, often listing names of churches and other organizations to whom they could write for help. As a result, thousands of prospective migrants wrote letters to black churches, such as the Bethlehem Baptist Association in Chicago, Illinois, which assumed the task of helping black migrants find housing and employment. They also helped migrants to adjust to their new environment." This information matches what can be learned from the letter itself. It is also possible to independently verify the letter's author and date, confirm that the external circumstances under which the letter was written are factual. Investigation such as this will help determine From a researcher's perspective, verifying where and when the document was written, determining whether or not witnesses were in a position to observe the events they recorded—and even better, whether or not the evidence provided by this witness is credible enough to support the hypothesis—is a singular achievement.

Given the endlessly subjective nature of our interpretations, thinking critically about the internal contents of a record becomes even more important. Many records are delivered to archives or libraries in preassembled collections with established provenance; certainly the Library of Congress is a model of reliable research on provenance. And today, more and more records are uploaded to archives' Web sites. This technological convenience has definitely eased and improved researchers' access to the materials, but it still doesn't mean that one can avoid a physical trip to the archive to examine the documents onsite. Most history writers who work with primary sources (as all should) reject the idea that good researchers would willingly exempt themselves from this particularly rich kind of analysis. Plus, reading documents closely is a treat. It's striking how often one finds something unexpected: maybe a handwritten note is scrawled in the margin of a typed letter, or maybe an old photograph is clipped to the document and was not considered worthy enough to be scanned for the Web site but turns out to be important to the research. Four questions will help researchers understand how they can turn the process of reading and interpreting the internal content of a document into reliably analyzed data:

1. What is the literal meaning of the document?

2. Does a specific bias or prejudice validate—or invalidate—the author's argument?

3. Can the trustworthiness of the author's conclusions be determined?

4. Does corroborating evidence seem essential to understanding the document?

To go back to Adams's letter to the Bethlehem Baptist Association, the literal meaning of the letter lies in the way it clearly conveys the harsh conditions of life in the South, and also the extent of her information about available assistance. Does Adams have a bias? Of course, and so does everyone else. But one needs to ask if this bias validates her argument. In Adams's case it does, since she is living under the conditions she reports. From verifying the dates, it can be determined that Adams is referring to her oppressed circumstances in early-20th-century Georgia. Since she was in Macon, she was in a position to report on circumstances in the city, and the researcher's general knowledge of American history confirms that Georgia compelled African Americans to a life of segregated poverty in more ways than many other parts of the country. This is evidence that corroborates the story in the letter. The evidence also shows that the historical question is not whether such evaluations are reasonable—historiography is crammed from book to book with biases each of which demands a strong response—but to what extent Mrs. Adams's letter is attuned to historical reality.

Analyzing Oral History Data

History emerges in a fascinating way when researchers listen to tapes or read transcripts in today's oral history collections. But the material alone is not sufficient for a study; researchers need to probe the interviews' contents for reliability and validity.

Oral history reliability lies in the consistency with which an individual or group can repeat the same story about the same event(s) on different occasions; if two accounts differ, to what extent is the narrator aware of the differences between the two? Informants who initially seem quite credible may be utterly unreliable. How accurate are their explanations and reminiscences? Interviewees sometimes "re-write" history, and without being aware, change the story after meeting the interviewer and shed a better (or worse) light on themselves or historical events than is accurate. Because of the inaccuracies of memory, oral history must be evaluated and judged for its accuracy as much as any other historical source, even documents found in an archive.

Interviewers themselves influence the course of the interview, often involuntarily. The interviewer is the designated persuader and theorist, sometimes causing interviewees to say what they believe the interviewer wants to hear. Silent nods, occasional objections, or resigned smiles while the interviewer waits to speak are signs that may inadvertently alter or add to memories. Even though the interviewer is recording the experiences of another person, what is created is a "shared authority" (Frisch, 1990). An interview is an interactive dialogue, with both people contributing to the recording of the account.

Validity, therefore, refers to the conformity between an oral report and data located in primary resource material such as documents, diaries, letters, or other oral reports. After conducting interviews, the researcher should attempt to locate whatever official records might be available to either corroborate or disprove the stories told by the informant. Other tests of validity include comparing witnesses (verifying the information from other, perhaps competing, witnesses) and determining the time and place of observations (the witness's proximity to the event) because, as Gottschalk writes (1969, pp. 150–155), "the closer the time of making a document of the event it records, the better it is likely to be for historical purposes."

In the coming years, it may turn out that the most important constituency applying pressure to social work history writers to merge oral history with their archival research will not be the oral historians themselves but rather the groups of psychoanalysts and postmodernists who are pursuing the newer intellectual arenas of narratology and narrative in research. With its origins in French structuralist thought of the 1960s and 1970s, narratology focuses explicitly on the internal components of a narrative's structure (words, imagery, sounds) and on how the relationship between these parts gives meaning to the narrative text. Invariably, this process enriches the interpretation of oral history data: on one level, researchers cull primary historical evidence from the story, but on a deeper level, they also explore the identity and social status of the narrator, the narrator's own consciousness of history, and perhaps the narrator's unconscious intentions in telling—or retelling—the story.

Analyzing Quantitative Data

Analyses of quantitative historical materials have provoked a lively debate concerning their validity and reliability. Quantification is best suited to material such as census data, voting records, or eligibility records. The validity of the quantitative approach has been criticized less for what it does than for what it omits: it overlooks historically significant data simply because they do not take easily to a quantitative form, and it assigns too much weight to factors that happen to be readily quantifiable (Heckathorn, 1983). The appeal of numbers, tables, and graphs is such that the limitations of this method can be easily obscured. In particular, it becomes less reliable when it strays too far from areas with preexisting countable data. In other words, displaying a hospital's admissions records in table form is fine since these data were recorded as numbers from the start. But attempting to do the same with patient narratives, for example, would have dubious reliability and validity.

Since quantitative data are generally marshaled from a variety of sources, their statistical analysis may seem problematic. Many primary data sources were never intended to be uniform or even comparable: few personal letters are identical, for example. But quantification need not be so cryptic even for letters. Once the researcher has identified the variables, the data capture instrument will arrange them in cells that can then be sorted or tabulated in any number of ways. Simple descriptive statistics, such as counts and percentages, can be combined with basic inferential tests to develop a compelling piece of an argument or to support (or disprove) a hypothesis.

Traditionally, the use of inferential statistics in historical research has been associated with random or other probability samples (Floud, 1975,

p. 173). However, many data are missing since we lack access to full historical populations or a probability sample of them, except for censuses, U.S. Department of Labor statistics, and relatively well-known elite groups whose statistics may be aggregated in social registers. Fortunately, imaginative investigators such as Gidon Cohen (2002, p. 170) offer good suggestions. "In scientific inquiry, much work has gone into the development of statistical methods to deal with 'observational' situations in which no probability sampling is possible and in which experiments cannot be done." Cohen suggests that stratification, subclassification, and samples of convenience can indicate interesting relationships between variables. And today, since most social work researchers are well-versed in the use of SPSS, applying quantitative techniques to qualitative data is losing its mystery.

Permission to Publish Data

Requesting Permission to Reproduce or Publish Material from Archives

Permission to obtain a copy of archival and manuscript material does not necessarily convey the right to publish or to reproduce the material. The researcher is responsible for obtaining permission from the holders of any rights in material being quoted, reproduced, or published. The library grants permission solely in its capacity as owner of the physical property. Therefore, publication privileges are secured only with the combined permission of the holder of the literary rights and of the library as owner of the material. The holder of the literary rights may be the writer, the writer's heirs or assigns, the writer's literary executor or other designated legal representative, the library itself, or the host university or government agency. Some permissions require a use or special handling fee. Short quotes, those that fall within the fair use guidelines of the United States Copyright law, do not require written permission from the library.

Most libraries ask researchers to submit written requests for permission to reproduce or publish material from rare books, manuscripts, or archival material owned by the libraries. If and when permission to publish is granted, applicants agree to state in their published citations, bibliographies, and credits where the original manuscript material is held. Most libraries ask the applicant to assume full and complete responsibility for such use and to defend and indemnify the institution against any claim, demand, cost, or expense related to any infringement of any literary rights, copyrights, or other rights that may result from use or publication of the archival and manuscript material held by the institution.

The request for reproduction or publication should include the following information:

- If the material is from a printed book, include the author's name, title, date and place of publication, full call number including collection name, and page number(s) or other identifier of the material requested. Example: frontispiece to *The Works of Horatio Walpole, Earl of Orford*, ed. Mary Berry (London, 1798), PR3757. W2A115 Rare), vol. 2, engraving of the Castle of Otranto.
- If the image is from the archival photo files, provide the full four-part image identification. Example: Series II, American Meat Institute, Laboratory, No. 1.
- If the image is from a digital collection on a Web site, give the unique image ID from that collection. Example: American Environmental Photographs, AEP-NYP7.
- If the material is from a document in a manuscript or archival collection, describe the item, its box and folder location, and the name of the collection. Example: Edith Jackson to Irmarita Putnam, letter of January 11, 1932, Series 3, Box 5, Folder 102, Edith Banfield Jackson papers, Schlesinger Library, Radcliffe Center for Advanced Study, Harvard University.

The request should also include the following information about the publication (or other media) where the requested material will appear:

- The author's name and title of the book or article in which the material will be published
- The name of the journal, book publisher, or production company if it is a film or CD

- The projected date of publication, performance, public presentation, or broadcast
- Whether the image(s) will be used in promotional material such as posters or other advertising
- If a broadcast, the network or cable channel on which the program will appear
- If a Web site, the URL and name of producer
- If a book, where the image(s) will appear: dust jacket, frontispiece, or text
- If a book or CD, the projected size of the press run, in numbers of copies
- If a book or CD, the projected retail price
- In books, language, area of distribution, number of editions, and size at which image will be printed may also be relevant.

Copyright and Fair Use Policies

Under U.S. law, copyright is a property right established by the Constitution to give the author/owner of original works the exclusive right to reproduce the copyrighted work, prepare derivative works, distribute copies by sale or other transfer of ownership, perform or display the copyrights work publicly, or authorize any of these. All others must respect the author's right of ownership over the work. Under the Copyright Act of 1976, however, the rights accorded to the owner of a copyright are subject to certain limitations, called "fair use" and "public domain," explicitly germane to research and scholarship. Works considered to be in the public domain are most U.S. government documents and works published more than 75 years ago. But works created in or after 1978 are copyright-protected for the life of the author plus 50 years, and works published between 75 years ago and 1977 and that bear a copyright notice are protected for 75 years from the date of publication. The terms for "fair use" are more ambiguous, and it is safest to request permission to publish or quote a source directly from the copyright holder, that is, the author or the author's estate. The guidelines do not specify an actual number of words, lines, or other elements that may be taken whole and without permission; tables always require permission. Nevertheless, common sense suggests that sentences may be quoted from academic articles and secondary sources (as I have done in this text) as long as they are appropriately cited and referenced. Most primary sources fall under copyright guidelines. Oral histories are considered primary sources; if the researcher has recorded the history and retains the signed release form, the narrative belongs to the researcher. Realia are generally deemed to be the property of the owner, and permission to publish photographs of objects must be secured from the owner.

Onward

Virginia Woolf found a challenge in history. Woolf's main object as a writer was to show that lack of information about the past hinders both the psyche and the transformative effect of critical inquiry. She struggled to keep us engaged on a deeper level, experiencing history as though it were happening not only to distant others but also to ourselves as architects of historical narratives as well. And so she issued a dare: "The more we believe, the less we know."

The methodology for writing history holds at least two additional lessons for social workers and others interested in improving individual and social conditions. First, at least in the realm of research, perseverance works. One way to get to the root of a social problem is to figure out how and where it emerged within a society—but also to do so from within that society's own narrative. At first archival and oral history research may seem intrusive, like poking around in a relative's secret stash of love letters, but it is in no way inconsistent with other research methods that investigate human and social problems. Conversely, we cannot assume that historical documents always tell the "truth" about a person or an event. If our goal is to improve truthfulness, the least a solid historiographic structure can do is to eliminate the illusion that we are telling the truth. It's a great place to start.

6

Historical Research Forms and Resources

Sample Interview Agreement (on Letterhead Stationery)

I hereby authorize (name) _____
to use my oral history memoirs, which were recorded on the following
date(s):

_____

_____

I understand that qualified scholars will be permitted to listen to the
tapes and use the interviews for their research. In addition, I wish to grant
qualified researchers my permission to use the materials in connection
with their research or publications, or for other educational purposes.

_____   _____
Signature of interviewee   Date

Address: _____

_____

Phone number _____

E-mail address _____

_____   _____
Signature of interviewer   Date

Address: _____

_____

Phone number _____

E-mail address _____

Restrictions:

Signed: _____

Interviewer Checklist

Interviewee: _____   Date: _____

_____ Tape recorder

Make sure:
1. Recorder is recording
2. Batteries (if necessary) are fresh
3. Power cord is available
4. Operating instructions are accessible

_____ **External microphone** (and fresh battery, if necessary)

_____ **Batteries** (if necessary)

       Backup set of new batteries

_____ **Audio- or videotape** (if necessary)

       Backup set

_____ **Extension cord** (12 feet) and adapters for two-pronged outlets

_____ **Four copies of interview agreement/release forms** (one for the subject, one for yourself, and two backups if needed)

_____ **Research notes and question sets**

_____ **Pre-interview questionnaire forms** (if used)

_____ **Addresses, phone numbers, and copies of correspondence with interviewees and other individuals who may accompany them, if necessary**

_____ **Notebook and pens**

Sample Letter to Prospective Subject

Your address and e-mail address

Date

Addressee name and address

Dear _____:

As a doctoral candidate at _____ University, I am writing to you in the hope that I might draw on your experience and involvement in the history of _____. My dissertation on the historical topic of _____ would greatly benefit from an interview with you.

[Insert brief description of the study].

My dissertation, conducted under the supervision of _____ University's School of Social Work, will combine archival research and oral history. Clearly, recollections from your own experience as a participant in the _____ would enhance this research. I hope that you will grant me an interview of an hour or so at your convenience.

I will call in several days to set up a time and place to meet. Looking forward to speaking with you then, I am,

Yours truly,

Sample Follow-up Letter to Subject

Your address and e-mail address

Date

Addressee name and address

Dear _____:

Thank you, once again, for sharing your experience of and involvement in the history of _____. My dissertation has benefited immeasurably from the interview with you.

I would now like to ask you to verify its content. You will find enclosed two identical copies of the typed transcript. Kindly read it over and on one copy correct spelling, names, dates, and anything else you wish. I will incorporate your corrections into my final paper. The second copy is yours to keep.

When you are finished, please call me at _____ or send me a note by e-mail. I will pick up your corrected paper in person, at your home or at your office, whichever is most convenient for you. Please do not send any original materials through the mail.

Thanking you once more for your generosity, I am,

Yours truly,

Social Work Archives and Special Collections

The following directory is organized alphabetically by name of archive. The individual listings contain names, addresses, contact numbers, Web site addresses, names and contents of the archives collections, and research grant availability; the data are up to date as of the publication of this book but are subject to change. This is not a comprehensive list, but it will give you a sense of the breadth and depth of primary sources available in the United States.

American Medical Association/Department of Archives
515 North State Street
Chicago, IL 60610
Phone/FAX: 312-464-4083 or 312-464-5130/312-464-4184
Email: Archives@ama-assn.org
Web site: www.ama-assn.org/ama/pub/category/1938.html
Collections: Historical Health and Alternative Medicine, Photographs, Memorabilia, Artifacts, Rare AMA Books and Publications, Films, Videos and Audio Tapes
Subjects: Documents, photographs, films, books, memorabilia, and artifacts document AMA initiatives and activities from medical ethics and medical education to clinical research, public health, and other professional issues.
Fellowship: No

American Red Cross/Hazel Braugh Record Center and Archives
7401 Lockport Place
Lorton, VA 22041
Phone/FAX:703-541-4601/800-989-2272
Web site: www.redcross.org/museum/exhibits/braugh.asp
Collections: Correspondence, publications, memoirs, oral histories, scrapbooks, photographs, video
Subjects: The corporate memory of the American Red Cross National Headquarters. Organizational records, library collection, still and moving

image materials. Subjects include disaster relief, blood donor program, nursing services, assistance to the military, health and safety, Junior Red Cross, and Red Cross and Red Crescent movement.

Fellowship: No

Binghamton University, SUNY/Center for the Historical Study of Women and Gender
Library Tower 606, Library Tower 606
Binghamton, NY 13902
E-mail: chswg@binghamton.edu
Web site: womhist.binghamton.edu, http://scholar.alexanderstreet.com/ display/WASM/Home+Page (Web site is under construction)
Collections: Audio recordings, books, images, journals, manuscripts, pamphlets, video recordings, oral histories and memoirs
Subjects: No comprehensive list of holdings.

1. Women and social movements in the United States, 1600–2000

2. Black Women Oral History Project: autobiographical memoirs of black American women who made significant contributions to American society in the early and middle decades of the 20th century, including Rosa Parks, Dorothy West, Jesse Abbott, Sadie Alexander, and Merze Tate.

Fellowship: Has calls for proposals for document projects

Chicago Historical Society/Research Center
1601 North Clark Street, Chicago, IL 60614
Phone: 312-642-4600
Web site: www.chicagohistory.org/research/aboutcollection
Collections: General collection arranged by name of person or organization
Subjects: Records of individuals, businesses, and organizations document life in Chicago, including early history, social conditions and problems, 20th-century neighborhood life, community organizations, African American history, ethnic history, women's history, civil liberties and civil

rights, politics, religious-centered social action, labor unions, environ-mental concerns, teachers, and school reformers.

1. Mary McDowell Settlement Records, 1894–1970 (bulk 1930–1962). Head resident of the University of Chicago Settlement. Letters, speeches, board minutes, reports, letters, and financial papers document the settlement's objectives, activities, and organization, and economic and social conditions in the Packingtown area. Labor conditions, unemployment, immigrant groups, recreational facilities and clubs at the settlement.

2. Chicago Commons Association Records, 1894–1979. Correspondence, minutes, annual and other reports, personnel records, records of clubs based at the settlement house, neighborhood census data and surveys. Topics include employment, housing, education, social conditions of neighborhoods, ethnic and racial neighborhood change and its problems, education for naturalization, interracial camping.

3. National Association of Social Workers, Illinois Chapter Records, 1921–1978. Correspondence, reports, minutes, and topical files of chapter founding, the professionalization of social work, standards and ethics of social workers, codes of conduct for welfare agencies, employment practices and personnel regulations, welfare legislation, public aid matters, conditions during the Great Depression and World War II, National Association of Social Workers, American Association of Group Workers, American Association of Medical Social Workers, American Association of Psychiatric Social Workers, and Chicago Round Table of Psychiatric Social Work.

Fellowship: No

Colorado River Indian Tribes Library/Archive
Rt. 1, Box 23-B, Parker, AZ 85344
Phone/Fax: 928-669-1332/928-669-8262
Web site: http://critonline.com/critlibrary
Collections: Arranged by topic

Subjects: Culture and history of the Colorado River Indian tribes. Original written documents, copies of documents, microfilm, photography, videotape and oral history tapes, personal correspondence, federal government documents, and works of historians, ethnologists, and anthropologists.
Fellowship: No

Columbia University/Oral History Research Collections
810 Butler Library, 535 W. 114th Street, New York, NY 10027
Phone/Fax: 212-854-7083
E-mail: oralhist@libraries.cul.columbia.edu
Web site: http://www.columbia.edu/cu/lweb/indiv/oral/index.html
Collections: Nearly 8,000 taped memoirs and 1 million pages of transcript
Subjects: War on Poverty, the student movements of the 1960s, the history of the psychoanalytic movement, women's history, and September 11, 2001.
Fellowship: No

Columbia University/Social Work Library Agency Collection
Lehman Library, 420 West 118th Street, New York, NY 10027
Phone/Fax: 212-854-5153
E-mail: rbml@libraries.cul.columbia.edu
Web site: www.columbia.edu/cu/lweb/indiv/socwk/guides/swagency.html
Collections: Manuscript, rare books, oral history, social work agencies
Subjects: Primary publications of domestic and foreign voluntary and public social service agencies, institutions, and organizations. General and annual reports, conference and workshop proceedings, position papers, and training and case documents document social work, social service, families and children, day care, aging, health and mental health, alcoholism and drug addiction, and social and physical rehabilitation.

1. Archives of the Institutions Endowed by Andrew Carnegie. Records of Carnegie Corporation of New York, Carnegie Endowment for

International Peace, Carnegie Foundation for the Advancement of
Teaching, and Carnegie Council on Ethics and International Affairs.

2. The Center for Human Rights Documentation and Research. Various
human rights organizations, including Human Rights Watch and
Amnesty International USA.

3. Viola W. Bernard Papers, 1907–1998. Psychiatrist, psychoanalyst,
child welfare advocate, and pioneer in the field of community
psychiatry. Correspondence, oral history interviews, reports, patient
records, photographs, audio and video recordings, phonograph records,
printed material, newspaper clippings, and artifacts.

4. Lillian Wald Papers, 1895–1936. Director of the Henry Street
Settlement in New York City. Papers and office files of the Henry Street
Settlement and philanthropic and liberal causes, including child welfare,
civil liberties, immigration, public health, unemployment, and the peace
movement during World War I.

5. Mary Richmond Papers, 1821–1928. Pioneer social worker, author,
and educator. Correspondence, manuscripts, and organizational records
document efforts to reorganize and introduce new methods, including
the case method.

6. Community Service Society Archives, 1842–1995. Correspondence,
reports, memoranda, case records, photographs and printed material,
central and district administrative records, committee correspondence
and minutes, program files, and casework files from the beginning of
social work.

Fellowship: No

Cornell University, Division of Rare and Manuscript Collections
2B Carl A. Kroch Library, Ithaca, NY 14853
Phone/Fax: 607-255-3530/607-255-9524
Web site: rmc.library.cornell.edu/collections/rmccollections.html
Collections: American history and culture; American Indian history and
culture; Latin American history and culture; photographs and visual

materials; popular culture; sexuality and gender; Southeast Asian history and culture

Subjects: Printed volumes, manuscripts, photographs, paintings, prints, and other visual media.

1. Samuel J. May Anti-Slavery Collection. Anti-slavery struggle at the local, regional, and national levels. Sermons, position papers, offprints, local Anti-Slavery Society newsletters, poetry anthologies, freedmen's testimonies, broadsides, Anti-Slavery Fair, pamphlets, letters on the progress of the Civil War, letters from the battlefield, maps, newspapers, prints, clippings, and pamphlets.

2. American Indian History and Culture. Manuscripts, missionary reports, ethnography, travel writing, native language dictionaries, captivity narratives, children's books, pamphlets, newspaper clippings, auction catalogs, newsletters, and travel brochures document native peoples of the Americas from the colonial period to the present. Indian lifeways, myths and folklore of Apache tribes; field notes from the Cornell-Peru project; contemporary politics, education, and human rights issues, biography files on prominent Native Americans.

Fellowship: No

Duke University/Rare Book, Manuscript and Special Collections Library
103 Perkins Library, Duke University, Durham, NC 27708-0185
Phone/Fax: 919-660-5820/919-660-5934
E-mail: special-collections@duke.edu
Web site: http://library.duke.edu/specialcollections/about/index.html
Collections: African and African American, documentary photography, gay and lesbian studies, newspapers, U.S. southern history and culture, utopian literature, women's history and culture
Subjects: History and culture of the American South and the experience of marginalized groups. Includes Confederate imprints, Civil War regimental histories, and southern broadsides; letters and diaries document politics, business, labor, education, religion, race relations, and other

aspects of life in the South from the antebellum period through the late 20th century.

1. Behind the Veil: Documenting African American Life in the Jim Crow South, Records, 1890–1997. Oral history of African American life during the age of legal segregation in the American South. Interviews and family photographs of black elders documents the crucial role that black churches, fraternal societies, women's clubs, and political organizations played in African American community life, the civil rights struggles in the 1960s, African American participation in desegregation within local communities, and post-1965 activism and community work.

2. Slave Letters. Holds some of the few in existence. Content varies and most have no supporting information about the author, but provide a glimpse into the lives of people who were enslaved.

3. Earnest Sevier Cox Papers, 1821–1973. Correspondence, writings, and printed materials of racial separatist and white supremacist include correspondence with Mittie Maude Lena Gordon, black founder of the Peace Movement of Ethiopia, and correspondence with Amy Jacques Garvey concerning the Back to Africa movement.

Fellowship: Yes

Georgetown University/Special Collections Lauinger Library
Washington, DC 20057-1174
Phone/Fax: 202-687-7614/202-687-7501
E-mail: scheetzn@georgetown.edu
Web site: www.library.georgetown.edu/dept/speccoll/index.htm
Collections: Archives, manuscripts, rare books, digital special collections
Subjects: American history; diplomacy, international affairs and intelligence; European history; political science

1. Harry L. Hopkins Papers. FDR's most trusted advisor. Appointment books, diaries; drafts of Hopkins's speeches and memoranda; photographs and drawings; and extensive correspondence.

2. The Carl A. S. Coan Collection in Housing and Urban Affairs, 1954–1976. Staff director for the Senate Subcommittee on Housing and Urban Affairs for over 25 years. Personal and professional papers, manuscripts, government documents, typescripts, and related items concerning housing, urban development, and mortgage credit that affected both domestic and international hosuing projects.

3. Daniel James Papers, 1960–1985. The collection comprises the extensive research files of historian Daniel James on Che Guevara, the Mexican Communist Party, and in general on Latin American and Caribbean poliitical affairs during the period 1960–1985.

Fellowship: No

Library of Congress/Manuscript Division
101 Independence Avenue, SE, Room LM 101, James Madison Memorial Bldg, Washington, DC 20540-4680
Phone/Fax: 202-707-5387/202-707-7791
Web site: www.loc.gov/rr/mss
Collections: Presidential papers, papers of government officials, organizational records, other papers, special collections
Subjects: Ten thousand separate collections include manuscript treasures of American history and culture.

1. National Urban League, 1918–1986. Correspondence, office memoranda, proposals, reports, speeches, press releases, contracts, financial records, organizational charts, directories, manuals, Urban League publications and other printed matter, minutes of meetings, awards, mailing lists, drawings, and radio transcripts.

2. Pioneers in Housing: An Oral History Project, 1981–1996. Documents development of public housing and community planning. Interviews with officials in the Department of Housing and Urban Development and its predecessor, the Housing and Home Finance Agency, educators in urban studies, and community developers.

3. A.Philip Randolph Papers, 1909–1979, and Records of the Brotherhood of Sleeping Car Porters, 1920–1968. Labor union official and civil rights leader. Correspondence and documents relating to presidential executive orders, memoranda, notes, printed matter, reports, scrapbooks, speeches, Brotherhood of Sleeping Car Porters, the Fair Employment Practices Committee, marches on Washington for employment and equal rights for African Americans, and the civil rights movement.

4. Susan B. Anthony Papers, 1846–1934. Correspondence, diaries, daybook, speeches, scrapbooks, and miscellaneous papers relating primarily to Susan B. Anthony's writings, lectures, and other efforts on behalf of women's suffrage and women's rights. Includes material pertaining to the National Woman Suffrage Association (after 1890 the National American Woman Suffrage Association) and to the New York State Woman Suffrage Association.

5. Sigmund Freud Papers, 6th century B.C.–1998 (bulk 1871–1939). Founder of psychoanalysis. Correspondence, holograph, and typewritten drafts of writings by Freud and others, family papers, patient case files, legal documents, estate records, receipts, military and school records, certificates, notebooks, pocket watch, Greek statue, oil portrait paintings, genealogical data, interviews, research files, exhibit material, bibliographies, lists, photographs and drawings, newspaper and magazine clippings, and other printed matter.

6. Wilhelm Reich Papers, 1920–1952. Pschoanalyst and physician. Correspondence, minutes, writings by Reich and others, explanatory notes by Reich, lists, programs, photographs, photocopies, transcripts, and translations of correspondence to and from Reich concerning the development of his theories, his break with Sigmund Freud and the psychoanalytic movement in 1934, and his involvement with communist and socialist movements in Austria and Germany during the 1920s and 1930s.

Fellowship: No

Michigan State University Libraries/The American Radicalism Collection
Special Collections, 100 Library, East Lansing, MI 48823
Phone/Fax: 517-432-6123 ext. 100
Web site: specialcollections.lib.msu.edu/index.jsp
Collections: Alternative press, Communist Party of the USA, Edith and
Arthur Fox Collection, Ku Klux Klan, American radicalism vertical file,
Saul Wellman Collection
Subjects: Books, pamphlets, periodicals, posters, and ephemeral material
on political, social, and economic issues in America with an emphasis on
radical groups, both left and right. Timothy Leary, the Black Panther
Party, neo-Nazi organizations, the Christian right, and Steve Gaskin;
publications from the American left in the twentieth century; American
labor history, the Ku Klux Klan, growth of American communism, and
the student anti-war movement of the 1960s; the contemporary men's
movement; and the gay and lesbian communities.

1. Alternative Press. Subscriptions, back files, and sample issues.
Publications of the political parties of the left and racist and neo-Nazi
organizations of the right, underground newspapers from the 1960s and
1970s, and advocacy and social change publications address women's
rights, the environment, gay and lesbian issues, alternative living,
United States foreign and domestic policy.

2. Communist Party of the USA, 1919–1950s. Materials from the
Communist Party of the USA, American Workers Party, the Communist
League of America, the Revolutionary Workers League, youth branches
and front organizations, and anti-communist materials from
governmental agencies and commercial publishers. Books, discussion
papers, policy questions and intraparty disputes, minutes of meetings,
and pamphlets.

3. Edith and Arthur Fox Collection. Political and labor activists in
Detroit. Pamphlets, election material, and shop papers that document
their involvement in a number of dissident groups within the United
Auto Workers and Trotskyite Socialist Workers Party, and internal party
material from the late 1930s to the Vietnam War era.

Fellowship: No

Minnesota Historical Society Library
345 Kellogg Boulevard West, St. Paul, MN 55102-1906
Phone/Fax: 651-259-3300
E-mail: reference@mnhs.org
Web site: www.mnhs.org/collections/about.htm
Collections: Archaeology, art, artifact, collections at historical sites, library, manuscript, map, moving images, music, newspaper, oral history, photograph, poster, state, state historical preservation office
Subjects: Chronicles Minnesota's history.

1. African Americans. Papers, photographs, maps, artworks, publications, and artifacts that document the history of Minnesota's peoples of color.

2. GLBT. Papers, photographs, artworks, publications, and artifacts that document the history of Minnesota's gay, lesbian, bisexual, and transgender citizens.

3. Hispanics. Papers, photographs, maps, artworks, publications, and artifacts that document the history of Minnesota's peoples of color.

4. Organized Labor. Diaries, correspondence, minutes, reports, newsletters, speeches, scrapbooks, bargaining files, and administrative files of local, state, and national unions, political parties, union and party leaders, activists, individual working people, and businesses.

5. Philanthropy. Records of philanthropic and charitable organizations, and the papers of many individual philanthropists.

6. Women. Personal diaries, non-current records of major organizations. Farmers, educators, artists, politicians, servants, homemakers, professionals, judges, environmentalists, writers, and others are represented from the anonymous to the famous, from 19th-century pioneers to 20th-century diplomats.

Fellowship: No

National Archives and Records Administration
700 Pennsylvania Avenue, NW, Washington, DC 20408-0001
Phone/Fax: 202-357-5400/301-837-0483

Web site: http://www.archives.gov/research
Collections: Searchable database by topic, format, agency or region
Subjects: Documents and materials record the history of the United States Federal government. The records and artifacts are held in NARA facilities around the country.

1. Records About Community Action Program Grants and Grantees, 1964–1981. Correspondence, memoranda, circulars, pamphlets, copies of applications for funds, reports on applications, and miscellaneous records relating to social welfare programs.

2. Office of the Federal Register. Provides access to the official text of federal laws, presidential documents, administrative regulations and notices, descriptions of federal organizations, programs and activities.

3. Main Photographic Print File of the Department of Housing and Urban Development, 1965–1995. Photographs documenting departmental activities and programs, housing, historic preservation, and urban renewal projects, including many well-known landmarks and neighborhoods where historic preservation was achieved through assistance from HUD.

Fellowship: No

New-York Historical Society
170 Central Park West, New York, NY 10024
Phone/Fax: 212-485-9225 or 212-485-9226/212-875-1591
Web site: https://www.nyhistory.org/web/default.php?section=libraryan dpage=reference_assistance_form
Web site: www.nyhistory.org/web/default.php?section=libraryandpage= collections
Collections: Printed, graphic, manuscript
Subjects: History of New York City and State; colonial history; the Revolutionary War; the Civil War; religions and religious movements, 18th and 19th century; the Anglo-American slave trade and conditions of slavery in the United States.

1. Newspapers. Published prior to 1820, original colonial New York papers, commercial and political dailies, and principal newspapers of the northern and southern cities during the Civil War.

2. Children's Aid Society Archives, 1853–1930. A new collection still being catalogued. Includes handwritten ledgers, surrender books, photos, and flyers advertising Orphan Train arrivals.

3. The Slavery Collection, 1709–1864. Correspondence, legal documents, and financial documents related to the North American slave trade, slave ownership, abolition, and political issues pertinent to slavery.

4. Records of the Association for the Benefit of Colored Orphans, 1836–1972. Meeting minutes, volumes recording indentures, administrative correspondence, financial records, admission and discharge reports, newspaper clippings, reminiscences, visitor registers, and building plans.

5. Records of the Emergency Shelter, 1928–1988 (bulk 1929–1975). History of a men's homeless shelter in Manhattan. Photographs, slides, brochures, flyers, scrapbooks, letters, articles, and reports.

6. Ladies' Christian Union Records, 1850–2001 (bulk 1858–1960). Provided affordable housing to young women in New York City. Documents 150 years of efforts to assist young women working and studying in New York City.

Fellowship: No

New York Public Library/Humanities and Social Sciences Library
Manuscripts and Archives Division, Fifth Avenue and 42nd Street, New York, NY 10018
Phone/Fax: 212-930-0801
Web site: http://www.nypl.org/research/eref/hssl/erefhssl.cfm
Web site: www.nypl.org/research/chss/index.html
Collections: General collection arranged by name of person or organization

Subjects: Date from the third millennium B.C. to the current decade. Documents, photographs, sound recordings, films, videotapes, artifacts, and electronic records.

1. American Fund for Public Service Records, 1922–1941. Nearly every progressive group active between 1922 and 1941 is represented among the Fund's applicants. Internal and external correspondence, meeting minutes, committee reports, and surveys.

2. Women's Prison Association of New York Records, 1845–1983. Correspondence, minutes, reports, legislative bills, project files, client case files, financial records, photographs, printed matter, reports, and fund-raising records. Client case records contain case books, rolls, registration cards, and samples of daily reports on residents of the Hopper Home.

3. Lillian D. Wald Papers, 1889–1957. Public health nurse, social worker, founded the Henry Street Settlement and the Visiting Nurse Service of New York. Correspondence, speeches, writings and collateral papers. Subjects include child welfare and labor, civil liberties, immigration, unemployment, housing, recreation, sanitation, prohibition, women's suffrage, and the peace movement during World War I.

Fellowship: Yes

New York Public Library/Schomburg Center for Research in Black Culture
515 Malcolm X Boulevard, New York, NY 10037-1801
Phone/Fax: 212-491-2200
E-mail: scmarbref@nypl.org
Web site: www.nypl.org/research/sc/sc.html
Collections: General collection arranged by name of person or organization
Subjects: History and culture of peoples of African descent, mostly in the Americas and the Caribbean. Personal papers, records of organizations and institutions, subject or thematic collections, broadsides, ephemera, and rare books cover the history, literature, politics, and culture of

peoples of African descent in the Americas, Africa, and England, primarily in the 20th century. Includes women in the United States; Haitian history; African American religion; the social, cultural, and political history of Harlem; education in Africa and the United States; civil rights organizations and activities; research files of scholars and intellectuals; and papers and records of individuals and organizations documenting radical political movements.

1. Rietta Hines Herbert Papers, 1940–1969. Documents the educational and professional development of a black woman in the field of social work, social work in general, New York State Department of Social Welfare and New York City Department of Welfare, Children's Placement Division.

2. The Olivia Pleasants Frost Papers, 1937–1994. A research consultant to numerous social organizations and educational institutions. Reports, proposals and memoranda from her work with New York Urban League, Harlem Mortgage Improvement Council, New York City Youth Board, Bedford-Stuyvesant Youth in Action, City University of New York, Metropolitan Applied Research Center, Columbia University, and Olivia Frost Research Associates.

3. James Weldon Johnson Community Centers, Inc. Records, 1942–1988. Board of directors minutes and committee files; executive director correspondence and subject files; program files; fund-raising records; and photographs. Documents social conditions, demographic change, political activity, philanthropy, and social work in East Harlem with a strong emphasis on the urban renewal period of the 1950s and '60s.

Fellowship: Yes

New York University/The Tamiment Library and Robert F. Wagner Labor Archives
70 Washington Square South, 10th floor, New York, NY 10012
Phone/Fax: 212-998-2630/212-995-4225
Web site: www.nyu.edu/library/bobst/research/tam
Collections: Library, archival, political, biographical manuscripts, archives of Irish America, non-print, oral history, vertical files

Subjects: History of the labor movement and relationship between trade unionism and progressive politics, New York City Central Labor Council's member unions, and the history of radical politics: socialism, communism, anarchism, utopian experiments, the cultural left, the New Left, and the struggle for civil rights and civil liberties.

1. Library Collections. Labor union convention proceedings, union journals, strike bulletins, underground newspapers, internal bulletins of radical organizations, scholarly journals, alternative press index, left index, and work-related abstracts.

2. Archival Collection. History of the left, the place of the worker in American society, the evolution of labor law, women's history, immigrant history, neighborhood associations, fraternal and ethnic societies, political organizations, and the unions.

3. Political Collections. Early local Socialist Party and predecessor organization records, the Rand School of Social Science, the Intercollegiate Socialist Society, the New York Bureau of Legal Advice (precursor to the ACLU), papers of Eugene V. Debs, Congressman Meyer London, Harry Laidler, William Mailly, and James Oneal, Rose Pastor Stokes, cartoonist Art Young, Michael Harrington, and Democratic Socialists of America. Activities of the Communist Party of the United States: its leaders, cadre, rank-and-file activists, and supporters, as well as records describing government investigations and prosecutions of the Communist Party and its members.

Fellowship: No

New York–Presbyterian/Weill Cornell, Medical Archives

1300 York Avenue, #34, New York, NY 10021-4805
Phone/Fax: 212-746-6072/212-746-8279
E-mail: ems2001@med.cornell.edu
Web site: www.med.cornell.edu/archives/about_us
Collections: Institutional archives, personal papers and manuscripts, patient medical records
Subjects: Records of the New York–Presbyterian/Weill Cornell and institutions that merged to form the current medical center represent a

continuous chronicle of health care, scientific research, and medical education dating back to 1771.

1. Institutional Archives. Records of New York–Presbyterian Hospital/ Weill Cornell Medical Center (formerly New York Hospital), Weill Medical College of Cornell University, and several other institutions that have merged or affiliated with the medical center are also available.

2. Personal Papers and Manuscripts. Manuscripts and papers of physicians, faculty, nurses, students, and administrators associated with the medical center. Topics include improving the health care of the Navajo people, family papers from the Civil War through World War II, diaries, and the recent history of AIDS and response of government and the medical community to the pandemic.

3. Patient Medical Records. Records from New York Hospital, Bloomingdale Asylum/Hospital, Lying-In Hospital of the City of New York, and several other institutions document the changes in patient population and medical/nursing care over a period of more than 200 years.

Fellowship: No

Oklahoma Historical Society
2401 North Laird Avenue, Oklahoma City, OK 73105-7914
Phone/Fax: 405-522-5225
E-mail: lmartin@okhistory.org
Web site: www.okhistory.org/res/ResDiv.html
Collections: Indian records, Indian-pioneer papers, photo archives, manuscripts, film/video, oral histories, maps, newspapers
Subjects: History of Oklahoma and its people.

1. Indian Archives Records, 1860–1930. Papers and volumes from United States Indian Agencies in Oklahoma and national records of the Cherokee, Chickasaw, Choctaw, Creek and Seminole Nations.

Fellowship: No

Radcliffe Institute/The Arthur and Elizabeth Schlesinger Library on the History of Women in America

10 Garden Street, Cambridge, MA 02138

Phone/Fax: 617-495-8662/617-496-8340

E-mail: radarch@radcliffe.edu

Web site: http://www.radcliffe.edu/schles

Collections: Manuscript/archival, books and periodicals, photographic and audiovisual, college archives

Subjects: Letters, diaries, and personal papers of women and families; records of women's organizations; books about women; cookbooks; women's periodicals; photographs; videotapes; and oral histories document women's activities in the United States and abroad from the early 19th century to the present day.

1. Elizabeth Prince Rice, 1948–1969. Personal papers and photographs, professional papers, reprints, conference papers, and lectures document development of social service departments in hospitals, social work techniques for physicians, social factors influencing child health, courses on the social service structure in hospitals and the interrelationship of health and welfare services.

2. Anna Seward Pruitt and Ida Pruitt Papers, 1860–1992. Correspondence, scrapbooks, diaries, and published and unpublished writings, social work case notes, speeches, minutes and correspondence from Indusco, writings of Rewi Alley, photographs and life in China.

3. Florence Ledyard Cross Papers, 1885–1961. Correspondence, manuscripts, scrapbooks, pamphlets, leaflets, clippings, and her journals document social work with immigrants in New York City and Rochester, New York, the National American Woman Suffrage Convention of 1916, suffrage work in Connecticut (1918), and her travels at home and abroad.

4. Molly Dewson Papers, 1893–1962. Correspondence, writings and speeches, programs, reports, minutes, clippings, and published works document Dewson's work with the American Red Cross in France, the National Consumers' League on minimum wage problems, the Democratic National Committee's women's division, the Women's

Educational and Industrial Union, Boston, and the Massachusetts
Industrial School for Girls, Lancaster.

5. Ethel Sturges Dummer, 1766–1962. Correspondence, speeches,
photos, reports, minutes, and articles document her work with juvenile
delinquents, prostitutes, and illegitimate children, progressive education
and Chicago public schools, and leaders of the mental hygiene
movement. Correspondence include Jane Addams, Havelock Ellis,
Sigmund Freud, Jessie Hodder, Karen Horney, Julia Lathrop, Norman
Thomas, Miriam Van Waters, and others.

Fellowship: Yes

Rockefeller Archive Center
15 Dayton Avenue, Sleepy Hollow, NY 10591
Phone/Fax: 914-631-4505/914-631-6017
E-mail: archive@rockefeller.edu
Web site: archive.rockefeller.edu
Collections: Rockefeller Family Archives, Rockefeller University Archives,
Rockefeller Foundation Archives, Rockefeller Brothers Fund Archives,
Rockefeller-related organizations, other nonprofit organizations
Subjects: The charitable organizations of the Rockefeller family. African
American history, education, international relations and economic devel-
opment, labor, medicine, philanthropy, politics, population, religion,
science, the social sciences, social welfare, and women's history.

1. Rockefeller Foundation Archives. Documents the life cycle of a grant.
Includes correspondence, institutional minutes, internal reports,
publications, officer diary excerpts, foundation grant actions, files on
refugee scholars escaping from fascist Europe, material relating to
public health, and correspondence documenting the foundation's
cooperation with the United Nations and U.S. government agencies.

2. Rockefeller Brothers Fund Archives, 1951–1989. Correspondence,
reports, memorabilia, grant actions, project files, correspondence,
memoranda, reports, financial records, and background material
relating to grant applications and grant administration. Documents

civic improvement, cultural advancement, education, health, religion, welfare, international relations and understanding, conservation, population, and racial equality in the United States and abroad.

3. Council on Foundations Records, 1949–1982. Early history of the Council, miscellaneous office and correspondence files, tax reform efforts in the late 1960s and early 1970s, Commission on Private Philanthropy and Public Needs' study of the scope and impact of charitable giving in the United States.

4. Russell Sage Foundation Records, 1907–1982. Correspondence, personal opinions, progress reports, daily activities, meeting agenda and minutes, progress and annual reports, financial statements, clippings, pamphlets and brochures. Subjects include education, juvenile delinquency, labor and industrial relations, penology, public health, recreation, social work, social work education, and urban and regional planning.

Fellowship: Yes

Roosevelt University Library/Center for New Deal Studies
430 S. Michigan Avenue, Chicago, IL 60605-1394
Phone/Fax: 312-341-3644/312-341-3499
E-mail: mgabriel@roosevelt.edu
Web site: www.roosevelt.edu/newdeal
Collections: Catalog of books, archival, Elizabeth Balanoff Labor Oral History, ephemera, David MacLaren Memorial Book Collection
Subjects: New Deal documented through archival collection, the ephemera collections, New Deal films and videos, and photographs.

1. Albert Lepawsky Papers. Includes summaries of interviews with almost 150 New Dealers, contemporary magazines and publications, sheet music, and unpublished studies of the New Deal.

Fellowship: No

Simmons College/Simmons College Archives and Special Collections Department
The Charities Collection, 300 The Fenway, Boston, MA 02115
Phone/Fax: 617-521-2440
E-mail: donna.webber@simmons.edu
Web site: my.simmons.edu/library/collections/college_archives/
charities_collections.shtml
Collections: College records, manuscript, photographs, historical books, charitable organization materials
Subjects: Personal papers, photographs, and memorabilia trace the training of women in nursing, social work, and teaching. Annual reports, pamphlets, and sermons of private charities, public welfare agencies, and hospitals in Boston, the eastern United States, and England from the 1790s to ca. 1950.
Fellowship: No

Smith College/Sophia Smith Collection
Alumnae Gym (Neilson Library), Smith College, Northampton, MA 01063
Phone/Fax: 413- 585-2970/413-585-2886
E-mail: ssc-wmhist@smith.edu
Web site: www.smith.edu/libraries/libs/archives
Collections: Administrative records, biographical records, audiovisual materials, manuscripts, photographs, periodicals
Subjects: Women's history from the colonial era to the present: birth control and reproductive rights, women's rights, suffrage, the contemporary women's movement, U.S. women working abroad, the arts, journalism and social work, and middle-class family life in 19th- and 20th-century New England.

1. Equal Rights Amendment Campaign Archives Program Records, 1970–1985. Correspondence, speeches, photographs, printed materials, interview transcripts, audiovisual materials, memorabilia, National Organization for Women's work to pass the Equal Rights Amendment, documentary footage from *Who Will Protect the Family* (based on the

1982 North Carolina ERA campaign) and *Fighting for the Obvious* (focusing on the Chicago, Illinois, ERA campaign).

2. Carel B. Germain Papers, 1922–1998 (bulk 1970–1995). Professor of social work focused on the ecological approach to social work theory and practice. Biographical information, writings, audio tapes of Germain teaching ego psychology, correspondence about teaching and the practice of social work.

3. Florence Hollis and Rosemary Ross Reynolds Papers, 1863–1987 (bulk 1930–1986). Social worker and professor. Correspondence, student papers, case records, writings and speeches, published articles, audio tapes, recordings, video tapes, agency records, photographs and oral histories documents.

4. Mary C. Jarrett Papers, 1900–1961. Psychiatric social worker, founder, and associate director, Smith College School for Social Work, professor, social work researcher. Research, writings, correspondence, formulation of the theory of psychiatric social work, United States Public Health Service and the Welfare Council of New York City.

5. Lydia Rapoport Papers, 1963–1968. Professor and social worker. Correspondence, lectures, published and unpublished articles, and research on family intervention, mental health consultation, and short-term casework.

6. Mary van Kleeck Papers, 1849–1998. Noted social reformer, lecturer, researcher, and writer. Documents her work in social and charitable agencies such as ACLU, National Woman's Party, Bryn Mawr Summer School for Student Workers, Hospites (a refugee rescue organization), the Women's International Democratic Federation, the Women's Trade Union League, and the National Research Council. Also the Russell Sage Foundation's Department of Industrial Studies, where she conducted investigations of the Rocky Mountain Fuel Company, United Mine Workers, and the coal industry, and her work with Mary Anderson at the Women's Bureau and Mary Fledderus at the International Industrial Relations Institute, 1925–1947.

Fellowship: Yes

Smithsonian Institution Archives
Washington, DC
E-mail: libmail@si.edu
Web site: http://www.sil.si.edu/research
Collections: Smithsonian Libraries; archival, manuscript and photographic collections
Subjects: The Smithsonian archives hold an estimated 50,000 cubic feet of paper documents, 7 million still photographs, and thousands of films and audio recordings

1. The Archives at the National Museum of the American Indian. Manuscripts, photographic images, and motion picture and audio recordings documenting contemporary and traditional lifeways and art of the native people of North, Central, and South America.

2. Human Studies Film Archives. Film and video collections of historical, archaeological, and ethnographic significance, including edited ethnographic films, unique research footage produced as part of anthropological research, and travelogues by amateur and professional filmmakers.

3. Ruth Koenig Mississippi Summer Project Collection, 1964–1966. A 23-year-old schoolteacher who volunteered for the Mississippi Freedom Summer in Holly Springs, Mississippi, which established a black political presence in the state of Mississippi, as well as organized various programs including the Freedom Schools and Community Centers. Includes personal and business correspondence, pictures, and various printed material.
Fellowship: Yes

Social Security Administration/SSA History Archives
Windsor Park Building, 6401 Security Boulevard, Baltimore, MD 21235
Web site: www.ssa.gov/history/archives/SSAGuideTOC.htm
Collections: Revolving files, flat files, bookcases, multimedia collections, lateral files, Mary Ross Papers, advisory councils and commissions, Schlabach Papers

Subjects: Programmatic, legislative, and administrative histories of Social Security and Medicare and the history of the Social Security Administration.

1. Revolving Files. Person files, subject matter files, and organizational files.

2. Mary Ross Papers. Longtime Social Security employee. Memoranda, congressional hearing reports, copies of multiple versions of developing legislation, and reports, studies, and booklets on a wide range of subjects document the most important developments in Social Security programs over the past 30 years.

Fellowship: No

Southern California Library for Social Studies and Research
6120 South Vermont Avenue, Los Angeles, CA 90044
Phone/Fax: 323-759-6063/323-759-2252
E-mail: archives@socallib.org
Web site: www.socallib.org/index.html
Collections: General collection arranged by name of person or organization
Subjects: Histories of communities in struggle for justice, labor, civil rights, women's, immigrants', and other grassroots movements.

1. Kristen Ockershauser Papers, 1965–1987. Community organizer, primarily documenting efforts in the early 1970s organizing residents in two public housing projects in the San Pedro area of Los Angeles.

2. Black Panther Collection, 1960s–1970s. Flyers, articles, ephemera documenting the Panthers in Los Angeles (and Oakland, California) and the library's run of the organization's newspaper, *The Black Panther*.

Fellowship: No

Swarthmore College Peace Collection
500 College Avenue, Swarthmore, PA 19081-1399
Phone/Fax: 610-328-8557/610-690-5728

E-mail: wchmiel@swarthmore.edu

Web site: www.swarthmore.edu/library/peace/peaceWeb site/scpcWeb site/Documents/frontpageAug2006.htm

Collections: Manuscript, audiovisual, book, periodical, photography, memorabilia

Subjects: Pacifism, women and peace, conscientious objection, nonviolence, civil disobedience, progressivism, the Vietnam era, African-American protest and civil rights, feminism, civil liberties, the history of social work, historic peace churches from the late 1800s to the present.

1. Jane Addams Papers, 1838– (bulk 1880–1935). Correspondence, Rockford Seminary notebooks, diaries, engagement calendars, writings and speeches by and about Addams, passports, visiting cards, reviews of her books, reference files, death notices, condolences, descriptions of memorial services, photographs, the Nobel Peace Prize medal, and memorabilia and personal library.

2. African Americans and Peace. Papers, audio, and video pertaining to civil-rights-era Freedom Marches, 1963 March on Washington, Committee on Race Relations in Philidelphia, anti-slavery and anti-lynching efforts, Congress on Racial Equality, and House Un-American Activities Committee.

Fellowship: Yes

Temple University/Samuel L. Paley Library Urban Archives
1210 W. Berks Street, Philadelphia, PA 19122
Phone/Fax: 215-204-8257 or 215-204-5750/215-204-3681
E-mail: urban@temple.edu
Web site: http://library.temple.edu/articles/index.jsp?bhcp=1
Collections: Books and pamphlets, newspaper clippings, manuscript, oral history, photographic, video, television, audiovisiual
Subjects: Social, economic, and physical development of the Philadelphia area from the mid-19th century to the present, social service organizations, unions, immigrant/ethnic communities, labor, politics and protest, senior citizens, women, housing development, community organizations,

and organizations involved with African Americans, education, and crime.

1. Fellowship House, 1931–1994. One of the earliest nonprofit education centers in human relations and social change. Organizational records and correspondence.

2. The Benjamin Feldman Series. Dedicated community activist. Organizing activities and inventory of neighborhood and regional groups active in Philadelphia and the Delaware Valley from the 1930s until the late 1970s; Feldman's defense against accusations of being a member of the Communist Party.

3. Charles L. Blockson Afro-American Collection. Books, manuscripts, pamphlets, journals, broadsides, posters, photographs, and rare ephemera document the history and culture of people of African descent.

Fellowship: No

The Institute for the History of Psychiatry/Oskar Diethelm Library
525 East 68th Street, Box 140, New York, NY 10021
Phone/Fax: 212-746-3728
Web site: www.cornellpsychiatry.org/history
Collections: Journal holdings, archives, and manuscripts
Subjects: History of psychiatry including psychology, psychoanalysis, mesmerism, hypnotism, spiritualism, phrenology, witchcraft, American mental hygiene movement, temperance movement, and religious and medical debates on witchcraft, suicide, and sexual behaviors. Psychiatric journals, early and rare first-person accounts of psychiatric illness, alcoholism, and drug abuse, hospital and asylum reports of the 19th and early 20th centuries.

1. Archives and Manuscripts. Unpublished papers and letters of many organizations and individuals vital to the history of psychiatry and the study of child psychiatry, psychoanalysis, the American mental hygiene movement, and biological psychiatry.

Fellowship: No

The Martin Luther King Center for Nonviolent Social Change/The King Center
449 Auburn Ave, Atlanta, GA 30312
Phone/Fax: 404-526-8983
E-mail: archives@thekingcenter.org.
Web site: www.thekingcenter.org/prog/research.html
Collections: Organizational records, manuscript, audiovisual, and oral history
Subjects: Papers of Dr. Martin Luther King Jr., the Southern Christian Leadership Conference, and civil rights organizations and notable individuals. Oral history interviews with Dr. King's teachers, friends, family, and civil rights associates.
Fellowship: No

The University of Illinois at Chicago/Library of the Health Sciences
Special Collections and University Archives, Room 320, 1750 W. Polk Street, Chicago, IL 60612
Phone/Fax: 312-996-8977
E-mail: http://www.uic.edu/depts/lib/digital/E-mailform.shtml
Web site: www.uic.edu/depts/lib/specialcoll
Collections: University Archives, Rare Books, Photography and Digital Images
Subjects: History of the health sciences.

1. Hull House Oral History Collection, 1974–2002. Reflect reminiscences of Jane Addams and the activities of the Chicago settlement house.

2. Hull House Collection, 1889–mid-1960s. History of Hull House from its founding.
Fellowship: No

The University of Illinois at Chicago/Richard J. Daley Library
Special Collections and University Archives, Room 3-330, 801 S. Morgan Street, Chicago, IL 60607

Phone/Fax: 312-996-2742
E-mail: http://www.uic.edu/depts/lib/digital/E-mailform.shtml
Web site: www.uic.edu/depts/lib/mainlib
Collections: Manuscripts, rare books, and photographs
Subjects: Records of individuals and organizations important to the history of Chicago.

1. Industrial Areas Foundation, 1952–2004. Correspondence, campaign materials, organizers' field reports, newspaper clippings, organizational publications, annual reports, and training materials under Saul Alinsky and Ed Chambers and the transitional period when the training institute originated and IAF activities became more institutionalized.

2. Edith and Grace Abbott Collection, 1909–1951. Residents of Hull House and founders of the Immigrants' Protective League. Articles, book reviews, newspaper clippings, yearbook, letters, memorials, reports, addresses, and writings.

3. Sophonisba Breckinridge Collection, 1912–1940s. Led the social work education movement in the United States. Correspondence, newspaper clippings, and articles.

4. Florence Kelley Collection, 1894–1981. Social worker, reformer, lawyer, suffragist, and socialist. Papers document residency at Hull House, formation of Chicago labor movement, the Intercollegiate Socialist Society, the National Association for the Advancement of Colored People in 1909, the Women's Peace Party, and the Women's International League for Peace and Freedom.

5. Julia Lathrop Collection, 1898–1921. Social worker and activist, helped create the Illinois juvenile court system. Articles, correspondences, newspaper clippings, writings, and speeches.

Fellowship: No

The University of New Mexico Center for Southwest Research
Zimmerman Library, 1 University of New Mexico, MSC05 3020, Albuquerque, NM 87131-0001
Phone/Fax: 505-277-6451

E-mail: cswrref@unm.edu

Web site: elibrary.unm.edu/cswr

Collections: Manuscripts, books, political archives, pictorial collections, Anderson Reading Room collection, university archives

Subjects: Political, economic and social history of New Mexico, the Southwest, and Mexico. Papers and records of politicians, historic and literary figures, architects, activists, attorneys, local families, organizations, and businesses. Correspondence, oral histories, scrapbooks, diaries, literary manuscripts, unpublished reports, financial records, legal documents, broadsides, maps, and audio/video recordings.

1. Sophie D. Aberle Papers, 1913–1987. Pueblo and Navajo Indians, general Native American issues, including relocation. Records from Aberle's tenure with the United Pueblos Agency, the Commission on the Rights, Liberties, and Responsibilities of the American Indian, and the National Science Board.

2. Robert L. Anderson American Indian Movement Papers, 1973–1996. Correspondence, news clippings, publications, audiocassettes, videotape, and memorabilia relating to contemporary Native American issues and prominent American Indians: FBI files, American Indian Movement (AIM), and individuals such as Leonard Peltier, Russell Means, Dennis Banks, Ward Churchill, Tim Giago, and Clyde and Vernon Bellecourt.

3. Alamo Navajo Oral History Project, 1977–1984. Interviews with people from the Alamo Navajo Reservation in southwestern New Mexico discuss Navajo kinship patterns, daily lifestyles, history and culture. Alamo revival meeting, and background research materials (project description, a master's essay on Alamo Navajo kinship systems, an ethnohistorical report on the Caoncito and Alamo Navajo bands, census data, and correspondence).

4. National Indian Youth Council Records, 1935–2000. Administrative and organizational issues and activities such as voting rights protection, American Indian religious freedom issues, political participation projects, treaty rights protection, public education, international work, and job training/placement.

5. New Mexico Office of Indian Affairs Records and Research Materials, 1936–ongoing. Correspondence, reports, audits, personnel records, publications and other administrative records, clippings, and documents pertaining to Indians of New Mexico and various state, regional, and national Indian organizations, including the All Indian Pueblo Council and materials pertaining to federal legislation concerning Indians.

6. Inventory of the Santa Fe Indian School: The First 100 Years Project, 1986–1987. Santa Fe Indian School students, employees, and teachers oral history interviews; transcripts; photocopies of photographs; the exhibition catalog; and assorted biographies, correspondence, and clippings from Pueblo people, Navajo, Apache, and non-Indian material addresses Indian student life, federal school policy, school adminstration, tribal and community involvement, and survival of Indian culture.

Fellowship: No

Tulane University, Amistad Research Center
Tilton Hall, Tulane University, 6823 St. Charles Avenue, New Orleans, LA 70118
Phone/Fax: 504-862-3222/504-862-8961
Web site: http://www.tulane.edu/~amistad/index.htm
Collections: Art, Archives and Manuscripts, Photographs, Digital Archives
Subjects: The nation's oldest, largest, and most prestigious independent archives specializing in African American history.

1. The American Missionary Association Archives. An abolitionist and interdenominational organization formed in 1846 from several early missionary groups. Most of the organization's founders were involved in the defense of the *Amistad* Africans from 1839 to 1841. It had a strong commitment to social justice and focused its efforts on abolishing slavery, assisting formerly enslaved people, improving the treatment of Native Americans, assisting immigrant populations, and meeting the needs of peoples in foreign lands. Between 1847 and 1865, the AMA

founded and/or supported 285 anti-slavery churches and commissioned
45 abolitionists as itinerant ministers in the United States. During and
after the Civil War, the AMA established hundreds of schools for
freedmen, including institutions of higher education such as Fisk
University, LeMoyne-Owen College, Atlanta University, Tougaloo
College, and many others. The organization's commitment to education
and social justice continued into the 20th century.

2. Save Our Schools Collection, 1957–1962. Save Our Schools was a
nonprofit organization established in 1960 by concerned parents and
citizens of New Orleans who wanted to maintain free statewide public
education in Louisiana during the integration era. Includes
correspondence, articles of incorporation, minutes, newsletters, reports,
and publications. The bulk of the collection consists of photocopies of
newspaper articles from 1960 to 1962.

Fellowship: No

University of Arkansas at Little Rock/Sequoyah Research Center
301A Ottenheimer Library, 2801 S. University Avenue, Little Rock, AR
72204-1099
Phone/Fax: 501-569-8336/501-371-7585
E-mail: dflittlefiel@ualr.edu or jwparins@ualr.edu
Web site: anpa.ualr.edu/default.htm
Collections: Bibliographies, digital library, manuscripts, *Cherokee
Phoenix* index, *Cherokee Advocate* index, Trail of Tears
Subjects: All aspects of life among American Indians, Alaska Natives, and
First Nations of Canada. American native press archives, contemporary
Native American newspapers, periodicals, and other publications; Native
manuscripts and special collections; press history, and literature.

1. *Cherokee Phoenix* Index. The first newspaper published by an
American Indian nation published the laws and public documents
of the Cherokee nation, relevant news of the day, and miscellaneous
information calculated to lead the Cherokees toward "civilization."

2. *Cherokee Advocate* Index. Published by the Cherokee Nation, 1844–1906. The only tribally owned and published newspaper in the country. Useful information for its Cherokee readers and accurate information regarding the Cherokees for its readers in the United States.

Fellowship: No

University of California, Berkeley/H. K. Yuen Social Movement Archive
Bancroft Library, University of California, Berkeley, CA 94720-6000
Phone/Fax: 510-642-6481/510-642-7589
E-mail: jberry@library.berkeley.edu
Web site: www.docspopuli.org/articles/Yuen.html
Collections: Collection is being processed. A collaborative project of UC Berkeley Ethnic Studies Library, Bancroft Library, UC Berkeley, and Institute for the Study of Social Change, UC Berkeley
Subjects: Social movements of the 1960s and 1970s. Multimedia primary documents from Free Speech Movement, Third World College mobilizations, United Farm Workers, student strike at San Francisco State University, Black Panther Party, American Indian Movement, International Hotel Mobilizations, Stop the Draft Week, women's movement. Organization flyers, underground newspapers, photos, posters, film, and early audio recordings of rallies, protests, debates and meetings. Pacifica network and community radio recordings, including documentaries, interviews, and live broadcasts.
Fellowship: No

University of Maryland/Archives and Manuscripts Department
University Libraries, 2208 Hornbake Library, College Park, MD 20742-7011
Phone/Fax: 301-314-2712/301-314-2709
E-mail: http://www.lib.umd.edu/special/research/contact.html
Web site: www.lib.umd.edu/special
Collections: Archival and manuscript, digital, government documents, media, rare and special book

Subjects: Personal papers and archival collections documenting Maryland history and culture, labor history, and women's organizations.

1. Archives of the Bureau of Social Science Research, 1950–1986. Correspondence, research notes, and reports used to plan social services (e.g., income maintenance and rural health care delivery services) for African American families and communities.

2. Archives of the Booker T. Washington Papers Editorial Project, 1967–1984. Office and business files, extensive correspondence, galley proofs, indexes, and biographical notes on persons who corresponded with Washington. This collection is unprocessed, but a preliminary inventory is available.

3. Archives of the Work Projects Administration in Maryland, 1933–1943. Records of the Maryland Work Projects Administration, Maryland Emergency Relief Administration, and the Civil Works Administration (CWA). Subjects include education and social welfare in Maryland.

4. National Public Broadcasting Archives. Record of the major entities of noncommercial broadcasting in the United States. Textual records, audio and video program records, and oral history tapes and transcripts from the NPR Oral History Project.

Fellowship: No

University of Michigan/Bentley Historical Library
1150 Beal Avenue, Ann Arbor, MI 48109-2113
Phone/Fax: 734-764-3482/734-936-1333
E-mail: http://bentley.umich.edu/bhl/refhome/refform.htm
Web site: bentley.umich.edu
Collections: Manuscripts, archives, photographs, and printed works
Subjects: History of Michigan.

1. Political and Social Reform and Activism. Manuscripts from people and organzations connected with political and social reform and activism in Detroit.

2. Arthur Dunham Papers, 1900–1980. Social worker in Massachusetts and Pennsylvania, professor of community organization at the University of

Michigan, pacifist imprisoned as a conscientious objector during World War I. Correspondence, subject files and research material, material on his pacifist activities, and published and unpublished writings.

3. School of Social Work (University of Michigan) Records, 1935–. Minutes, correspondence, curriculum records, and topical files.

Fellowship: Yes

University of Michigan/Labadie Collection
Special Collections Library, 711 Harlan Hatcher Library, 7th floor, Ann Arbor, MI 48109-1205
Phone/Fax: 734-764-9377/734-764-9368
E-mail: special.collections@umich.edu
Web site: www.lib.umich.edu/spec-coll/labadie/labadie.html
Collections: Photographs, archives and manuscripts, subject vertical file, 19th-century French political trials
Subjects: Social protest literature and political views from the extreme left and the extreme right. Anarchism, civil liberties (with an emphasis on racial minorities), socialism, communism, colonialism and imperialism, American labor history through the 1930s, the IWW, the Spanish Civil War, sexual freedom, women's liberation, gay liberation, the underground press, and student protest.

1. National Transgender Library and Archives. Books, magazines, films, videotapes, journals and newspaper articles, unpublished papers, photographs, artwork, letters, personal papers, memorabilia, and ephemera related to the transgender and transsexual condition.

2. American Committee for Protection of Foreign Born Records, 1926–1980. Founded in 1933 to defend constitutional rights of foreign-born persons in the United States. Correspondence, administrative files, clippings and publicity files, subject files and case files document efforts to aid individuals facing deportation or seeking to become naturalized citizens, and efforts to address harassment, discriminatory legislation, and official persecution.

Fellowship: No

University of Minnesota/Social Welfare History Archives
320 Elmer L. Andersen Library, 222 21st Avenue South, Minneapolis, MN
55455
Phone/Fax: 612-624-4377/612-624-4848
E-mail: d-klaa@umn.edu
Web site: special.lib.umn.edu/swha
Collections: National association records, personal papers, local agencies, pamphlet, related books and periodicals, gender
Subjects: Organizational records and personal papers document birth
control, sterilization, illegitimacy, prostitution, and venereal disease,
child welfare and family relations, community planning, recreation, settlement house movement, arts programs, preventive health, analysis of
public social policy, and interaction between private- and public-sector
programs.

1. Margaret Berry Papers, 1937–2001. Unofficial historian of the
settlement movement. Personal papers, clippings, memorials and
memorabilia document Social Service Employees Union, individuals,
social welfare organizations, and local, national, and international
settlements.

2. Benjamin E. Youngdahl Papers, 1916–1968. Public welfare
administrator and social work educator. Personal and professional
papers, and correspondence with Harry Truman, Adlai Stevenson,
Hubert Humphrey, and John F. Kennedy.

3. Child Welfare League of America Papers, 1900–2003. Minutes,
memoranda, reports, correspondence, conference programs,
publications, and professional standards, newsletters and bulletins,
National Association of Day Nurseries, and National Children's Home
and Welfare Association.

4. The Jean-Nickolaus Tretter Collection in Gay, Lesbian, Bisexual and
Transgender Studies. Books, unpublished manuscripts, vertical files, and
periodicals cover all time periods. Includes the National Education
Association GLBT Caucus, the *Lesbian Review of Books* archive,
Gay/Lesbian Postal Employees Network (PEN) of Minneapolis/St. Paul,
Paper Eagles (employee group of the Minneapolis *Star Tribune*,

the Ramsey County GLBT Employees Network, and the archives of the Twin Cities–GLBT Pride Committee.

5. Henry Street Settlement Papers, 1933–present. Minutes, correspondence, memoranda, reports, publications, financial records, newspaper clippings, photographs, maps, and newsletters document the administration and programs. Topics include immigrants and low-income groups, the arts, child care, camping and youth activities, health care, mental health, senior citizen programs, consumer education, juvenile delinquency, employment programs, adult education, and services for the homeless.

Fellowship: Yes

University of North Carolina at Chapel Hill, Manuscripts Department
Manuscript Department, 4th Floor, Wilson Library CB 3926, UNC Chapel Hill, Chapel Hill, NC 27514-8890
Phone/Fax: 919-962-1345/919-962-3594
E-mail: www.lib.unc.edu/mss/mailref.html
Web site: www.lib.unc.edu/mss
Collections: Southern historical collection, southern folklife collection, university archives, general manuscripts
Subjects: Diaries, journals, letters, correspondence, photographs, maps, drawings, ledgers, oral histories, moving images, albums, scrapbooks, and literary manuscripts document southern history, literature, and culture.

1. First-Person Narratives of the American South. Diaries, autobiographies, memoirs, travel accounts, and ex-slave narratives written by southerners, including those whose voices were less prominent in their time, including African Americans, women, enlisted men, laborers, and Native Americans.

2. North American Slave Narratives. Books and articles document the individual and collective story of African Americans in the 18th, 19th, and early 20th centuries. Includes all existing autobiographical narratives of fugitive and former slaves published as broadsides, pamphlets, or books in English up to 1920. Biographies of fugitive and former slaves and fictionalized slave narratives published in English before 1920.

Fellowship: Yes

University of Southern California/California Social Welfare Archive (CSWA)
Doheny Memorial Library 335, Los Angeles, CA 90089-0182
Phone/Fax: 213-740-2587 or 213-740-4035
E-mail: czachary@usc.edu
Web site: www.usc.edu/libraries/archives/arc/libraries/cswa/index.html
Collections: Agency and miscellaneous papers, CSWA oral histories, correspondence, minutes, memoranda, annual reports, research papers, conference proceedings, and newsletters
Subjects: History and diversity of social welfare in California, with an emphasis on southern California. Records of California social welfare and related organizations, development of social welfare programs, problems, issues, and services in the state, personal papers, roles of philanthropic groups, history of marginalized groups, benevolent societies, and religious groups.

1. Jessie E. Dean Papers, 1916–1943. First trained social worker to practice in Los Angeles. Professional papers, instructional training outlines for "visitors" and student social workers, County Welfare Division annual reports, essays on social welfare conditions, journals, reprints, pamphlets, articles, sermons, seminar notes and transcripts, reports, teaching materials, book excerpts and outlines, and intake forms from the Depression.

Fellowship: Yes

Wayne State University/Walter P. Reuther Library
The Archives of Labor and Urban Affairs, 5401 Cass Avenue, Detroit, MI 48202
Phone/Fax: 312-577-4024

E-mail: reutherreference@wayne.edu

Web site: www.reuther.wayne.edu/collections/alua.html

Collections: Unions, labor and urban affairs, university archives, oral history, audiovisual

Subjects: American labor movement, industrial unionism, and related social, economic, and political reform movements in Detroit and the United States.

1. Collections of the United Farm Workers of America. Papers of Cesar Chavez chronicle his work and leadership in the agricultural migrant labor organizing movement (1959–1993) and the United Farm Workers Union.

2. Cesar Chavez Oral History Interview, Robert F. Kennedy Oral History Program of the Kennedy Library, January 28, 1970. Cesar discusses his first meeting with Robert Kennedy as well as his work with the United Farm Workers Organizing Committee

3. United Automobile Workers Collection. Documents the history of automobile workers and their union.

4. American Federation of Teachers Collection. Includes personal records of notable leaders and local union records

Fellowship: No

Relevant Journals

Academic journals are excellent secondary sources. They are generally peer-reviewed periodicals that publish original research and scholarship, or that critique existing research in the form of articles, review articles, and book reviews. Fortunately, many of the articles in these journals are now available in full text online and are accessible through university libraries.

> *Access History*
> *Action Research*
> *American Historical Review*

American Journal of Psychoanalysis

American Journal of Psychology

American Journal of Public Health

Ankara Papers

Archival Science

Archivaria: The Journal of the Association of Canadian Archivists

Archives and Museum Informatics

ARL: Association of Research Libraries

Behavioral and Social Sciences Librarian

British Journal of Social Work

Bulletin of the History of Medicine

Canadian Social Studies

Cataloging and Classification Quarterly

Clinical Social Work Journal

College and Research Libraries

Columbia Journal of Historiography

Community Mental Health Journal

Comparative Studies in Society and History

Congressional Quarterly Researcher

Continuity and Change

Cromohs: Cyber Review of Modern Historiography

Cross-Cultural Research

Cultural and Social History

Cultural Studies, Critical Methodologies

Ethnohistory

European History Quarterly

Families in Society

Gender and History

Historian

Historical Journal

Historical Materialism: Research in Critical Marxist Theory

Historical Methods

Historical Research: The Bulletin of the Institute of Historical Research

Historically Speaking

Historiography East and West

History
History: Reviews of New Books
History and Memory
History and Theory
History of the Family
History of the Human Sciences
History of Psychiatry
History of Psychology
Innovation in Social Sciences Research
International Journal of Heritage Studies
International Journal of Mental Health
International Journal of Psychoanalysis
International Labor and Working Class History
International Review of Social History
Journal for Multimedia History
Journal of Behavioral Health Services and Research
Journal of Broadcasting and Electronic Media
Journal of Colonialism and Colonial History
Journal of Contemporary Ethnography
Journal of Contemporary History
Journal of Family History
Journal of Global History
Journal of Interdisciplinary History
Journal of Mixed Methods Research
Journal of Modern History
Journal of Narrative Theory
Journal of Policy History
Journal of Social History
Journal of Social Service Research
Journal of Social Studies Research
Journal of Social Work Research and Evaluation
Journal of Sociology and Social Welfare
Journal of the American Academy of Child and Adolescent Psychiatry
Journal of the American Planning Association
Journal of the Association for History and Computing

Journal of the History of the Behavioral Sciences
Journal of the Oral History Society
Journal of the Society of Archivists
Journal of Urban History
Journal of Women's History
Journal of World History
Library of Congress Information Bulletin
Limina: A Journal of Historical and Cultural Studies
Magazine of History
Martyrdom and Resistance
Mental Health Services Research
Narrative Inquiry
Oral History Review
Organizational Research Methods
Organization of American Historians Magazine
Past and Present
Perspectives American Historical Association
Phylon: The Atlanta University Review of Race and Culture
Political Psychology
Psychiatric News
Psychoanalytic Social Work
Public Historian
Qualitative Health Research
Qualitative Inquiry
Qualitative Report Qualitative Research Journal Quality and Quantity
Radical History Review
Research in Public Policy Analysis and Management
Research Strategies
Resources for Feminist Research
Rethinking History
Review of Policy Research
Reviews in History
Science and Society
Signs: Journal of Women in Culture and Society
Smith College Studies in Social Work

Smithsonian
Social Policy Journal
Social Research
Social Studies
Social Science History
Social Science Journal
Social Science Quarterly
Social Work
Social Work Research
Sociological Methods and Research
Studies in Qualitative Methodology
Transcultural Psychiatry
Urban History

References

Abbott, C., & Adler, S. (1989). Historical Analysis as a Planning Tool. *Journal of the American Planning Association, 55,* 467–473.

Abramovitz, M. (1996). *Regulating the Lives of Women: Social Welfare Policy from Colonial Times to the Present.* Boston: South End Press.

The African-American Mosaic. (1993). A Library of Congress Resource Guide for the Study of Black History & Culture. Ed. Debra Newman. Washington, DC: US Library of Congress

Addams, J. (1910). *Twenty Years at Hull House.* New York: Macmillan.

Barker, R. L. (1998). *Milestones in the Development of Social Work and Social Welfare.* Washington, DC: NASW Press.

Barrow, F. (2007). Forrester Blanchard Washington and His Advocacy for African Americans in the New Deal. *Social Work, 52 (3),* 201–208.

Barzun, J., & Graff, H. (1992). *The Modern Researcher,* 5th edition. Boston: Houghton Mifflin.

Bell, J., ed. (2002). *Biographical Dictionary of Industrialization and Imperialism, 1880–1914.* Westport, CT: Greenwood Press.

Bernstein, M. (2001). The Great Depression as Historical Problem. *Organization of American Historians Magazine, 15 (4),* 1–15.

Berry, C. (2000). *A Confederate Girl: The Diary of Carrie Berry, 1864.* Mankato, MN: Blue Earth Books, a division of Capstone Press

Bormann, E. B. (1969). *Theory and Research in the Communication Arts.* New York: Holt, Rinehart and Winston.

Bremner, R., et al. (1970). *Children and Youth in America: A Documentary History.* 3 vols. Cambridge, MA: Harvard University Press.

Breton, M. (2002). Empowerment Practice in Canada and the United States: Restoring Policy Issues at the Center of Social Work. *Social Policy Journal, 1 (1)*, 19–34.

Bullard, A. (2005). L'Oedipe Africain, a Retrospective. *Transcultural Psychiatry, 42 (2)*,171–203.

Carlton-LaNey, I., & Burwell, N. Y., eds. (1996). *African-American Practice Models: Historical and Contemporary Responses.* New York: Haworth.

Romanovsky, P. (1978). *Social Service Organizations.* Westport, CT: Greenwood Press.

Chauncey, G. (1994). *Gay New York: Gender, Urban Culture, and the Making of the Gay Male World.* New York: Basic Books.

Cohen, G. B. (1984). Ethnic Persistence and Change: Concepts and Models for Historical Research. *Social Science Quarterly, 65*, 1029–1041.

Cohen, G. (2002). Missing, Biased and Unrepresentative: The Quantitative Analysis of Multisource Biographical Data. *Historical Methods, 35 (4)*, 166–176.

Craver, K. W. (1999). *Using Internet Primary Sources to Teach Critical Thinking Skills in History.* Westport, CT: Greenwood Press.

Davies, K. (1996) Capturing Women's Lives: A Discussion of Time and Methodological Issues. *Women's Studies International Forum, 19 (6)*, 579–588.

D'Emilio, J. (1998). *Sexual Politics, Sexual Communities: The Making of a Homosexual Minority in the United States 1940–1970, 2nd edition.* Chicago: University of Chicago Press.

Denzin, N. K., & Lincoln, Y. S., eds. (1998). *Strategies of Qualitative Inquiry.* London: Sage Publications.

Dunaway, D. K., & Baum, W. K., eds. (1984). *Oral History: An Interdisciplinary Anthology.* Nashville, TN: Oral History Association.

El Saadawi, N. (1994). *Memoirs from the Women's Prison.* Berkeley: University of California Press.

Elton, G. R. (1965). *The Practice of History.* New York: Thomas Crowell.

Eustace, N. (1993). When Fish Walk on Land: Social History in a Postmodern World. *Journal of Social History, 37*, 75–91.

Fausto-Sterling, A. (2000). *Sexing the Body: Gender Politics and the Construction of Sexuality.* New York: Basic Books.

Fisher, R. (1999). Speaking for the Contribution of History': Context and Origins of the Social Welfare History Group. *Social Service Review, 73 (2)*, 191–217.

Fisher, R., & Dybicz, P. (1999). The Place of Historical Research in Social Work. *Journal of Sociology and Social Welfare, 26 (3)*, 105–124.

Fixico, D., ed. (1997). *Rethinking American Indian History.* Albuquerque: University of New Mexico Press.

Floud, R. (1975). *An Introduction to Quantitative Methods for Historians.* London: Methuen.

Franklin, J. H. (1989). *Race and History: Selected Essays, 1938–1988.* Baton Rouge: Louisiana State University Press.

Furay, C., & Salevouris, M. (2000). *The Methods and Skills of History: A Practical Guide,* 2nd edition. Wheeling, IL

Frisch, M. (1990). *A Shared Authority: Essays on the Craft and Meaning in Oral and Public History.* Albany: State University of New York Press.

Garraghan, G. J. (1946). *A Guide to Historical Method.* New York: Fordham University Press.

Gay. P. (1998). *Freud: A Life for Our Time.* New York: W. W. Norton.

Gelbart, N. R. (1998). *The King's Midwife: A History and Mystery of Madame du Coudray.* Berkeley: University of California Press.

Godfrey, D. G. (2002). Broadcast Archives for Historical Research: Revisiting the Historical Method. *Journal of Broadcasting and Electronic Media,* 46 (3), 493–503.

Goldman, E. (1977). *Living My Life.* New York: New American Library.

Gottschalk, L. (1969). *Understanding History: A Primer of Historical Method,* 2nd edition. New York: Alfred A. Knopf.

Grele, R. J. (1987). On Using Oral History Collections: An Introduction. *Journal of American History,* 74, 570–578.

Harman, D., ed. (2007). *The Cambridge Companion to Narrative.* New York: Cambridge University Press.

Heckathorn, D. D. (1983). Formal Historical Analysis: Quantitative and Nonquantitative Approaches. *Social Science Journal,* 20, 1–16.

Hill, M. R. (1993). *Archival Strategies and Techniques.* Qualitative Research Methods no. 31. Thousand Oaks, CA: Sage Publications.

Hudson, P. (2000). *History by Numbers: An Introduction to Quantitative Approaches.* London: Arnold.

Judd, C. M., Smith, E. R., & Kidder, L. (1991). *Research Methods in Social Relations,* 6th edition. New York: Holt, Rinehart and Winston.

Kelly-Godal, J. (1976). The Social Relation of the Sexes: Methodological Implications of Women's History. *Signs: Journal of Women in Culture and Society,* 1, 809.

Kovel, J. (1988). *The Radical Spirit, Essays on Psychoanalysis and Society.* London: Free Association Books.

Laird, J. (1995). Family-Centered Practice in the Postmodern Era. *Families in Society,* 76 (3), 150–162.

Lambe, P. (2003). An Introduction to Quantitative Research Methods in History. *Journal of the Association for History and Computing,* 6 (2), 1–11.

Leiby, J. (1978). *A History of Social Welfare and Social Work in the United States.* New York: Columbia University Press.

Leighninger, L. (1987). *Social Work: Search for Identity.* Westport, CT: Greenwood Press.

Lorenzini, M. (2007). *New York Rises.* New York: Aperture.

Lubove, R. (1995). *The Professional Altruist: The Emergence of Social Work as a Career, 1880–1930.* Cambridge, MA: Harvard University Press.

Lubove, R. (1968). *The Struggle for Social Security, 1900–1935.* Cambridge, MA: Harvard University Press.

Magnússon, S. G. (2006). Social History as "Sites of Memory"? The Institutionalization of History: Microhistory and the Grand Narrative. *Journal of Social History, 39* (3), 891–913.

Margolin, L. (1997). *Under the Cover of Kindness: The Invention of Social Work.* Charlottesville: University of Virginia Press.

McLennan, G. (1986). Marxist Theory and Historical Research: Between the Hard and Soft Options. *Science and Society, 50,* 85–95.

Neustadt, R., & May, E. (1986). *Thinking in Time: The Uses of History for Decision-Makers.* New York: Free Press.

Olson, N. B. (2001). Cataloging Three-Dimensional Artefacts and Realia. *Cataloging and Classification Quarterly, 31 (3–4),* 139–150.

Palevsky, M. (2002). Questioning History: Personal Inquiry and Public Dialogue. *Oral History Review, 29* (2), 69–74.

Palombo, J. (1994). Incoherent Self-Narratives and Disorders of the Self in Children with Learning Disabilities. *Smith College Studies in Social Work, 64* (2), 129–152.

Pardeck, J. T., Murphy, J. W., & Choi, J. M. (1994). Some Implications of Postmodernism for Social Work Practice. *Social Work, 39 (4),* 343–346.

Piven, F. F., & Cloward, R. (1971). *Regulating the Poor: The Functions of Social Welfare.* New York: Pantheon.

Robyns, M. C. (2001). The Archivist as Educator: Integrating Critical Thinking Skills into Historical Research Methods Instruction. *American Archivist, 64,* 363–384.

Roehner, B. M., & Syme, T. (2002). *Pattern and Repertoire in History.* Cambridge, MA: Harvard University Press.

Ross, E. (1976). Black Heritage in Social Welfare: A Case Study of Atlanta. *Phylon: The Atlanta University Review of Race and Culture, 37* (4), 297–307.

Sands, R. G. (1996). The Elusiveness of Identity in Social Work Practice with Women: A Postmodern Feminist Perspective. *Clinical Social Work Journal, 24 (2),* 167–186.

Schick, J. B. M. (1990). *Teaching History with a Computer.* Chicago: Lyceum.

Schorske, C. (1980). *Fin-de-Siècle Vienna: Politics and Culture.* New York: Alfred A. Knopf.

Scott, J. W. (1986). Gender: A Useful Category for Historical Analysis. *American Historical Review, 91 (5),* 1053–1075.

Scott, J. W. (1991). The Evidence of Experience. *Critical Inquiry, 17 (3),* 773–797.

Simon, B. L. (1994). *The Empowerment Tradition in American Social Work: A History.* New York: Columbia University Press.

Simonton, Dean K. (2006). Presidential IQ, Openness, Intellectual Brilliance, and Leadership: Estimates and Correlations for 42 U.S. Chief Executives. *Political Psychology, 27 (4),* 511–526.

Steckel, R. H. (1991). The Quality of Census Data for Historical Inquiry: A Research Agenda. *Social Science History, 15 (4),* 579–599.

Tavakoli-Targhi, M. (2001). *Refashioning Iran: Orientalism, Occidentalism and Historiography.* New York: Palgrave Macmillan.

Tomlinson, C. (1996). Sandor Rado and Adolf Meyer: A Nodal Point in American Psychiatry and Psychoanalysis. *International Journal of Psychoanalysis, 77 (pt. 5),* 963–982.

Welshman, J. (1999). The Social History of Social Work: The Issue of the "Problem Family," 1940–70. *British Journal of Social Work, 29 (3),* 457–476.

Woolf, V. (1941). *Between the Acts.* London, England: The Hogarth Press

Wenocur, S., & Reisch, M. (2002). *From Charity to Enterprise: The Development of American Social Work in a Market Economy.* Urbana: University of Illinois Press.

Index

Printed in the USA/Agawam, MA
November 25, 2019

743521.004